BRIDGE OF DEMARCATION—
An Atlanta Odyssey

A White Student's Education in a Black University in the 1960s
A True Story by Duane and Loretta Johnson

CAPTIONS FOR PHOTOS

AJC FLASHBACK PHOTOS

Construction of the Hunter Street Viaduct being built in 1961 (now MLK Jr. Drive) while massive railyards take up the right side of the photo. Christened as 'Bridge of Demarcation' in September 1967.

Traffic Congestion on Downtown Atlanta Connector in 1967

West Hunter Street Baptist Church (huge gray-stone church 3 blocks from Ware Hall dormitory) (Pastor Ralph Abernathy April 7, 1968)

CONTENTS

Prologue

This book traces my experiences as a white man attending a black graduate school in 1967 and 1968, when the ill winds of prejudice in race relations were evident, and still remain. Repugnant to minorities and touted as a miserable failure, the melting pot axiom was a major weapon during the Civil Rights Movement of the 1960s.

The story begins when, as a graduate student from Montana, I was named a Sargent Shriver Fellow, which allowed me to attend an all-black college, Atlanta University, during the height of the Civil Rights Movement. I was shocked when I arrived and learned what this experience would entail. My journey began with the culture shock of seeing more black people than I had ever seen before. I was awestruck by the food, the outspoken prejudice of the southern whites, and the discrimination I witnessed towards blacks. Living in an all-black dorm was the backdrop for my initiation. My ignorance slowly turned to understanding as I learned with the help of fellow students and professors of my own racism. Civil rights and the turbulence are woven together as I confront the issues of the time.

During the summer of 1967, filled with hope and optimism after graduating with a bachelor of arts degree in sociology, I met the love of my life. We had known each other for six weeks and had only four dates when Loretta left to begin student teaching in a nearby town. After completing her student teaching assignment, she returned for her senior year at Montana State University. I wrote nearly fifty letters to Loretta between

September 1967 and July 1968. Her decision to keep her fifty-year-old love letters kindled my desire to look back at my graduate school experiences.

I experienced a range of emotions from revulsion and rejection to acceptance and endearment. Among the hate-filled stares, threats, and confrontations, I still found much more evidence validating our similarities rather than the differences between black and white cultural values.

In 1988, Atlanta University merged with Clark University and is now known as Clark Atlanta University, a leading private, historically black doctoral research university.

The language depicted throughout is reflective of the language used in 1967 and 1968. The fact that it is uncomfortable is a testament to how wrong we now believe that once-accepted behavior to be.

1

The White Perspective

I stare out the window as the prop jet surges through the clouds toward a place I've never been. Unaware at the time the journey would be an odyssey that would change my entire life. My thoughts drift back to my mother's kitchen the evening I opened and read the telegram from Senator Mansfield's office:

```
Duane STOP
Senator Mansfield is pleased to announce you as a
recipient of a fellowship to attend graduate studies
offered by Atlanta University. STOP
The fellowship will provide financial support for the
cost of tuition, fees and living expense stipend. STOP
Contact Dr. Cothran of the Sociology Department at
Atlanta University for details. STOP
Notice of acceptance must be received by Dr. Cothran by
September 10, 1967. STOP CONGRATULATIONS. STOP
```

"Duane, you're surely not going down to that God-forsaken part of the country," wailed my mother with her typical Scandinavian pessimism.

My mind reflected on the many times my checkbook balance dropped to zero while I scrambled to pay my college tuition while getting my BA, "You bet I'm going! Who else is going to pay for me to continue my education? This is a once in a lifetime opportunity!" My response could have been predicted after years of choosing to go against the grain of my overly protective parent. Standing barely five feet two inches, the matriarch was a feisty bantam weight that had long ago lost the upper hand in dictating her only son's life activities.

"Now, don't be foolish. Haven't you been watching TV? They are taking police dogs after those niggers[1] who are trying to break the color line. It's worse than a civil war. Some of them are carrying baseball bats and guns."

"Awe Mom, don't overreact. First, I will be going to graduate school and most colored people don't even go to college. I'll be miles away from those sit-ins and marches. And if I haven't learned how to stay out of trouble by now, it's too late for you to worry about it." I consider telling her that she is a racist but I know my 53-year-old Mother born in Saskatchewan, Canada is set in her beliefs.

I saw the same television news reports and can't say they didn't raise the same amount of anxiety in me as they had in my mother. I find myself vacillating between racial hatred for those who dared to confront the established norms and institutions. Then, I am seized by feeling sympathy, shame, and regret that whole groups of people are being denied access to schools, restaurants, and the political process just because of the color of their skin. It is easy to convince myself that it is not my concern; it is all so far removed from Montana. It's like another country; another political system.

I spent more time wondering how I ended up with this prized opportunity. I think, this time I won't have to work. This time I'll have time to read and contemplate the wealth of knowledge in my chosen discipline.

1 The language depicted throughout is reflective of the language used in 1967 - 68. The fact that it is uncomfortable is a testament to how wrong we now believe that once-accepted behavior to be.

Receiving a MA in Industrial Sociology will allow me to continue my fight for the underdog. I worry that I haven't been asked to write essay responses, and have passed exams by filling in the blanks that were facilitated by hours of mindless memorization. Do I have the ability to think and solve problems, to participate in research and adequately articulate results that can be useful?

After I call Mansfield's office, the first thing on Monday morning, I call Frank Hayes and tell him of my good fortune. I ask him, "Do you know how I got placed in such an opportunity?" Frank was my supervisor at the Hill County Community Action Head Start program and also the nephew of Senator Mansfield.

He immediately assures me, "I know all about it and I submitted your name as a budding young mercenary in the War on Poverty that could enhance his contribution by further education." He encourages me to "Go for it!" This is a ticket to the big time. No more nickel and dime state politics. This could mean a job with the Senior Senator himself. Besides, if it doesn't work out, Frank said he'd try to keep a slot open for me in his program.

During a change of planes at Chicago O'Hare, I end up sitting next to a heavyset man in his early 40s, who's dressed in a summer suit that suggests he's a traveling salesman. He orders two of the single-shot bottles of scotch being served by the stewardesses. Meanwhile, I drink a beer to help settle the growing tension in my stomach caused by the lurching and bumping of the plane as it barrels through an ever-increasing density of clouds. My beer goes down quickly and I begin to squeeze and turn the empty beer can, making a crinkling noise just barely audible over the roar of the plane's straining engines.

My scotch-and-water drinking fellow traveler lights a cigarette and announces, "It's always this way on Fridays."

I turn from staring out of the window and acknowledge his declaration with a silent nod. Not receiving any response from the woman seated on his left, he turns to me and adds, "I mean the Friday flights are always crowded and it takes them forever to serve us. That's why I always order two at a time. You never know if they will come around a second time."

"Makes sense to me—I thought you were talking about the weather. Is it always this bumpy?" While I'm not really in a talkative mood, I'm glad to engage in anything that will distract me from the bouncing and rolling of the plane.

"Oh no, but this time of year, you can expect some disturbance from the thunderstorms they have up here. This here storm is a pretty good one. You know the game in St. Louis was rained out today. That'll give them an extra day's rest when they come to Atlanta. I told my wife we aren't going to any more games until the Braves can get some decent pitchers. They don't want to use any of the boys from around the area but are willing to spend all sorts of money on players from outside of Georgia."

I don't closely follow baseball until the World Series launches, so I'm not sure what he's referring to but I pick up on his disdain for players that aren't from Georgia in his otherwise soft drawling speech. Not wanting to reveal my ignorance for the national sport of baseball but hoping to continue this distraction from the air turbulence, I try to steer the discussion to something of more immediate interest to me. "Any chance of being rained out in Atlanta tomorrow?"

"Oh, I hardly believe so. I called the wife before leaving Chicago and she says it will be a beautiful day and the forecast is supposed to continue through the weekend. She says it's going to stay right around eighty degrees. She's talking about wanting to drive over to Six Flags. She's always eager to go someplace the minute I get off the plane when all I want is to get some good home-cooked meals and settle down and stay put. I tell her she should take my place for a couple of weeks and she'd find out that traveling, eating in restaurants, and sleeping in strange beds is no picnic. But you know it doesn't do any good when she feels cooped up the way she is. You know she doesn't drive and she won't take the bus since they started letting them Nigras[2] take over."

"How do you mean?" I ask, thinking to myself, *I have never heard them called Nigras.*

"What do you mean how do I mean?' Don't you know you can be sitting and minding your own business and some Nigra might decide to sit right beside you and rub up against you. Especially them young ones; they are the pushy ones. No, I agree with my wife, it's just not safe anymore."

"What are you afraid of, being robbed?"

"Well it might come to that. Mostly they stink and carry all sorts of diseases."

"What kind of diseases?" I have not heard of his concerns but admit to myself that I am only aware of about half a dozen Blacks at Malmstrom Air Force Base and Great Falls does not have any city buses.

"What kind of diseases? Well, don't you know almost every one of them is carrying consumption and worse? That's what the stink is about in the eating places. It doesn't have to do with them being bad people, some are very nice, but they all are carrying diseases that they seem to be immune from but white folks aren't. That's why whites don't want to be around them that much not that they are all bad people. You wait and see, if another Catholic gets in the White House and keeps it up, our kids are all going to have polio and consumption."

Trying to stay on safe ground, I ask, "Atlanta your home?"

---

2 The language depicted throughout is reflective of the language used in 1967 – 1968. The fact that it is uncomfortable is a testament to how wrong we now believe that once-accepted behavior to be.

5

"Well it is and it isn't. I was raised in Grangeville, Georgia. But the company moved me to Atlanta because that's where all the action is. Atlanta is growing by leaps and bounds, mostly as a result of Yankees coming down to get good jobs. By the way, where are you from?"

"Montana." And then as if that was too general an answer and not having anything else safe to say, I add, "Great Falls, Montana, you know, right on the Missouri."

"Oh, hell yes, I've been to Billings. Montana's got good people— nothing like them Yankees from up North. What are you going to be doing in Atlanta?"

"I'm going to graduate school."

"Well that's mighty fine. Georgia's got a fine education system and we play damn good football, but you don't look like you're gonna be going to school on a football scholarship. How come you chose Georgia State, boy?"

I am saved from answering and I'm sure my response will turn off my new friend. We receive a further reprieve from the discomfort of flying by the stewardess asking if we want anything else to drink.

"Yes, two Dewar's with water, no ice and give my friend another beer," hurried the southern sales representative, disregarding the fact that the lady in the aisle seat had not yet responded.

When she does, she orders a Coke with ice and then takes me off the hook, joining in the conversation, "Well, I think it's just grand that some of you Northerners come and learn from us Georgia folk. You know we have a very rich culture in the performing arts as well as in literature. But our boys are awfully good at sports too." The last observation is seemingly offered to pay tribute to the older leader of the heretofore two-sided conversation.

"Here, let me pay for this round," I offer after no effort has been made to pay the stewardess who is standing anxiously counting a fistful of money, separating the singles from the fives from the tens. I reach for and open my wallet that has been tucked away in my rear pocket.

The salesman acknowledges, "Well that's mighty nice of you."

I try to locate a $10 bill from among the $20s in the wad of money cramming my full leather wallet. I sold my car and paid off all my outstanding debts before leaving Great Falls, and I'm carrying my entire net worth. That amounts to $940. It looks like a lot more than it is and I slowly thumb through the wad knowing that three sets of eyeballs are perceptibly watching. The stewardess is showing much more interest in the exchange than usual. I hand the stewardess a $10 spot and get one five and two ones back with a silky soft, "Thank you," before she pushes her cart and continues asking in a much more mundane tone, "Anything to drink?"

"That looks like some load of cash you're carrying young man. I'd be mighty careful not to flash it around much in Atlanta. There are a lot of people in Atlanta who won't blink before they come between you and that money—especially since you're a Northerner and all. I think it's safe to say that some Latinos hold Yankees in the same light as they do pushy Nigras. Yes son, they would split your skull open and claim that money faster than the twinkle of a lightning bug." His voice seems to gain in octave as he unfolds his amazed reaction to my handheld bankroll. "I would get right to a bank or put it in a hotel safe rather than be carrying that much money."

The Coke-sipping matron who looks like she is a middle-aged librarian in her summer suit agrees. "The gentleman is right. Sadly, there is a growing element in our city that would take your life for a lot less than what you have in your billfold."

Feeling embarrassed at my foolish effort to impress two people that I don't even know, I meekly acknowledge, "I'll be okay."

Mercifully, the NO SMOKING sign blinks on and the pilot instructs everyone to prepare for landing and that we are gracefully cleared for a straight on approach. The stewardess hurriedly comes through gathering cups and requesting our seat backs be returned to their upright positions. The conversation is squelched while each of us quickly gulp the last of our drinks.

The next word spoken is by the salesman as we are taxiing toward our gate. "Do you need a lift downtown?" And then as much for our woman companion who is staring blankly ahead, he adds, "I live on North Peachtree. My wife and I would be glad to drop you off downtown."

Remembering the expostulation on what some elements of Atlanta would do for the kind of money I am carrying, I don't think twice and lie, "No thanks, I have someone picking me up."

I'm happy that there's no sign of either of my seating companions as I claim my two bags. One's a military duffel bag full of clothes and the other is a hard-sided suitcase full of books. The sweat on my brow from lugging the two bags breaks out into a full-body swelter as I leave the air-conditioned airport and reach the sidewalk in front of a line of taxis. The air is akin to walking into a steam room. My shirt instantly sticks to my perspiring body and I feel the cool trickle of sweat run down in places I've never sweat before. My God, heat is one thing but this mugginess is something else. Oh well, it's September and things will cool off soon enough if I don't suffer a heat stroke first. Not sure how people can function without air-conditioning. Who in the hell could concentrate in this unearthly torridness? I hope I can make it!

"Taxi sir?"

"Yes, please a nice downtown hotel with air-conditioning," I unthinkingly utter, revealing that here is a damn Yankee with a bankroll in his pocket who has no idea where he is going.

"How would the Atlantan Hotel do you sir? It's in about the center of downtown Atlanta. Not too far from the railroad station and plenty of nice restaurants."

I become convinced that I'm getting ripped off when after a forty-five-minute ride the cabby says the charge is $4.50. I'm thinking, *Wow, things are going to cost a lot more in this huge sprawling city than I ever thought to pay back in Montana.*

The hotel promotes that it's completely air-conditioned, has television, and there's an invitation to visit the magnificent Persian cocktail lounge. I settle into my room as my mind wanders to Loretta, the tall, thin, green-eyed blonde with the luscious lips that I left behind in Montana.

September 13, 1967

Hi Sweet Pea,

Well, I got here safe and sound. I had real good connections all the way. But I still feel heat! But before I hit the sack, I will say a few good words to a little princess in Fort Benton, Montana.

I got here too late to try and make connections at the University. Hope to reach someone there that can help me get settled tomorrow.

This city is really spread out for only having a little more than a million people. It took 45 minutes to get to the hotel from the airport. It cost $4.50! Wow! I will have to take that into consideration when making it home at Christmas.

A fellow on the plane clued me that they dislike Yankees more than Negroes in Atlanta. So, guess I will have to pick up a "y'all" in my vocabulary.

It is very humid here. The temperature is only about 79 degrees but I feel like I'm sopping wet and I'm not sweating. Ugh! Muggy feeling.

Sweet Pea (Lorreta spelling?), I am going to miss you very much. I only hope that you will still be available when I get home. You have so much going for you that I feel frustrated leaving you. But if there was true sincerity in our friendship (and I believe there is) I am not going to sing the blues just because we are separated for a while. Oops – getting sentimental, am I not?

What the heck! I just want to say – I still do!!!

Kid…I'm tired and am writing pretty sloppy. Will try again after a day's rest and maybe I can let you know what's happening here.

Love you all,
Dew

2

A Shocking Discovery!

I breakfast in a restaurant about two blocks up the street from the hotel. I order an egg omelet with toast, a glass of grapefruit juice, and coffee. There's a glob of something served right alongside of the omelet. When the waitress returns to refill my coffee and ask if everything is okay, I ask, "What's this?" I look at her and point to the glob and experience my first Southern reaction to a Northerner.

The fortyish slightly overweight, blue-eyed waitress stares at me and her broad smile fades into a sneer as she coolly states, "That's grits, boy." Then almost as an act of forgiveness, she lazily quips, "Eat them, they'll put hair where you don't need it."

After she walks away, I shove a forkful into my mouth and slowly chew it as I try to identify something in my past diet that I can compare it to. It is tasteless except for the grease it absorbs from my egg omelet. The closest it comes to is a cereal my mother used to make on weekends called cream of wheat. Partly because I'm still hungry and partly because of my upbringing which demanded cleaning everything off a plate put in front of you.

She returns with the coffee pot and asks, "More coffee?"

"No ma'am, I wonder if I could have some brown sugar."

"We ain't got brown sugar. You want white sugar? It's on the table."

"No, I need brown sugar." Seeing her quizzical look, I add, "It's for them," pointing at the nearly untouched serving of grits.

"Boy—where you from? I've seen some y'all Yankees put salt and pepper on grits and I even had one bunch who put ketchup on them but I never heard of anyone who put brown sugar on them."

"Montana. I'm from Montana."

"Well, I can get you some ketchup if you want, but we don't got any brown sugar." With that she goes behind the counter and busies herself telling four separately seated men (all about her vintage look and age and all slightly overweight and then some) about the guy in the booth that wants brown sugar for his grits.

I felt somewhat redeemed when I hear a wisecrack from one of the big guys, "Hell, that sounds like it might be alright. I could take my grits with a little sugar. Heaven knows that is the only way you can get any sweetness around here."

"Now, you know that's not true," says the waitress. She's still carrying on with the counter customers when I stand in front of the cash register waiting to pay my tab. She hardly stops with the banter as she comes over and stares at me and then at where I sat and had my breakfast. A deep wrinkle develops between her penciled eyebrows and I can't help but look back to where I'd been seated.

I blush at the nearly untouched grits sitting on my plate with no gratuity alongside it. I know that's what's provoked the scowl as she thumbs through her order tickets and sweetly asks, "Your omelet all right?" Without waiting for a response, she rings up my bill and stuffs the $5 bill I hand her into the cash register and then freezes as she waits for my response.

"Oh yes ma'am, it was just fine."

She takes a few minutes figuring out my change and then hands me four quarters, a dime, and a nickel. And again, ever so sweetly she turns her attention to me and drawls, "You come back, hear."

I leave the dime, nickel, and a quarter on the rubber mat alongside the cash register and smile broadly as I turn to make my retreat to the street.

The sun is bright as I walk back toward the hotel. There is a slight breeze that cools the midmorning concrete citadel. More people are on the streets and most of the stores and shops have opened. I pick up my pace and decide that I won't wait until Monday to find my way around campus. I'm sure the campus will be every bit as big as this city and I don't want another scene whereby my lack of Southern culture is the cause of embarrassment. I'll spend the day getting acquainted with the geography of the campus and find out where the dorms are in relation to the classrooms. Maybe I'll spend some time in the library.

There is a solo cab parked in front of the Atlantan Hotel. I look up and down the street and don't see any other taxis so I decide to go now and avoid calling for a taxi later. I walk up and stick my head in the open window of the passenger side of the cab. "Would you take me to Atlanta University?" I ask, because I think the cabby might already be spoken for by someone inside the hotel.

"You mean Georgia Tech or one of the Georgia State schools. You might mean Emory University but I don't know if there is such a school as Atlanta University."

"Would you wait right here—I think the address is in my room. I'll go get it," I hurriedly answer, worried that I might be making an unreasonable imposition on the driver.

"Go get it. I'll bet you either want Georgia Tech or Georgia State," the driver counsels as he flips the flag up on his meter.

13

I take the steps two at a time and reach the hotel entrance then go through the lobby to the elevator. Inside the elevator, I hit my floor number and then rattle the CLOSE DOOR button thinking of the ungodly $5 hit the ride in from the airport cost me. My hand shakes in my haste and miss the damn key hole as I attempt to enter my room. Once in the room, I open the suitcase of books where I remember stashing the telegram from Senator Mansfield. Inside a hardbound copy of *Webster's New World Dictionary*, I find the yellow envelope and carefully peruse the printed message inside. I panic realizing that there's no address given for Atlanta University but then regain a sense of composure when I reread the telegram and note that it does state ATLANTA UNIVERSITY. I clutch the telegram and race out, leaving the suitcase open on the unmade bed. As I approach the taxi, I thrust the telegram into the open taxi window and reassert, "It says here, Atlanta University. Do you know where it's at?"

I didn't understand what the driver mumbled as he motioned for me to get in. Sitting on the edge of my seat, clutching my cabled ticket to a higher education, I notice that the meter has reached seventy cents. Concerned that the driver has assessed some special fee for the location of Atlanta University, I politely ask, "I beg your pardon?"

We're pulling away from the curb, and the driver is looking intently at the traffic-free street and barks, without looking back at me, "Boy, that's a nigger[3] school."

The driver's assertion sets me back in my seat. My head spins while I try to make some sense of what I've just heard. The words were spit out with clear contempt. We travel south several blocks in silence. A left turn takes us by some industrial warehouses and some railroad tracks. We come to a red stoplight and the driver puts on the right-turn blinker. When the light

---

3 The language depicted throughout is reflective of the language used in 1967 – 1968. The fact that it is uncomfortable is a testament to how wrong we now believe that once-accepted behavior to be.

turns, we turn and approach a bridge with multiple lanes of two-way traffic. The bridge is a railroad overpass, which is later christened as the "Bridge of Demarcation" when I'm able to put some order to the day's activities.

There are cars coming toward us driven by people of color. There are colored women as well as colored men driving every make and year of car imaginable. I realize this is the first time I've ever seen a colored person drive a car and quietly acknowledge that it's no big deal. We cross the bridge and make our way along a street with more people than I have ever seen on one street before. And they are all colored. Women in dresses, women in slacks, women in shorts, tall women, short women, thin women and fat, really fat women. I see children, some in strollers, some holding the hands of other children, and some being led by adults. There are children on bicycles and roller skates. There are men in suits, men in short-sleeves, men in bib overalls. I've never seen such a diverse collection. The one common denominator; they are all colored. I feel like I've been transported to some faraway foreign country. Even in my most vivid imagination, I could not dream of such a sight.

Unthinkingly, I blurt, "Wow, there's sure a lot of colored people over here."

The driver half-heartedly and half-disgustedly acknowledges my self-evident observation, "We have our share of them, all right."

The remainder of the ride is in silence. We go only a couple of blocks on the main drag past a huge church and then take a left. We drive about four blocks through a residential area with homes tucked behind a canopy of huge shade trees. My head is still spinning from culture shock. A strange sense of adrenaline pulsates through my body as the driver pulls in front of a two-story brick building that very much fits the image of an institution of higher education or maybe a hospital. I pay the $2 fare and when the driver seems to hesitate, I ask, "Do you mind waiting a few minutes until I see if this is the place?"

"You asked for Atlanta University. You got Atlanta University. I got other things to do." I watch as the taxi drives to the end of the block and makes a U-turn and returns up the street on the same route as we had just taken. The driver looks down at something on his seat as he goes by, avoiding eye contact with me. Whether I want to flag him down or not is now a moot question. He either has taken offense by the lack of a tip or he truly has other much more pressing business to attend to. His business with me is conclusively terminated.

I turn and walk up the wide sidewalk toward a building entrance with a sign that reads ADMINISTRATION in gold letters across the single door which serves as the main entrance. As I approach, I am drawn along a sidewalk that veers off to the left toward another red brick building that looks like it might be a classroom. Driven by past experience, I believe this must be the building that houses the faculty offices. I walk up and try the door only to find it locked. I turn to see if anyone has observed my failed attempt but no one's within earshot nor is anyone paying attention to this weekend visitor. I turn and walk further into the campus and spot a building designated the School of Business and Economics and wonder which building the office of a Dr. Cothran would be located.

The next building has several steps leading up to double doors. It could almost pass for a courthouse but approaching, I see it is the Graduate School Library. Pushed by more of a desire to escape the blinding sun than any sense of adventure, I feel fortune is with me when I find the door unlocked. I quietly enter and am overwhelmed with a sense of serenity. I can smell the wisdom of thousands of books and feel the presence of academia in the haunting emptiness. The library smells strongly of a mixture of aging leather, cloth, paper, and ink. I linger for several minutes and then start getting nervous that someone might question my presence in this port of literary wealth. I exit, push through the door and down the steps, quickening my pace to give my wandering a sense of purpose.

I double back to the Administration Building. Entering, I'm met with a musty and cleaning detergent odor. I hear the clatter of typewriters to my right. There is no one visible in the dimly lit hallway but a swath of light reveals an open door. I walk into a large, open office space and nine women busily typing on long scrolls of paper about the size of an index card. I sense that they're aware of my presence but the typing continues uninterrupted by even a sideway look in my direction. I straighten and clear my throat. Still not the slightest bit of acknowledgement. I don't know how long I stand there but again I'm overwhelmed by a light-headed dizziness and about ready to get the hell out of this building, city, state.

"Yes, do you need some help?" The words are spoken with more of a challenge than an offer of assistance from a young woman about my age. She is peering down her nose and over a pair of granny spectacles at me as she removes one roll of whatever they are typing on and inserts yet another. No one else appears to be aware of the exchange.

"Ah, yes ma'am, I think I'm lost," I answer honestly referring to my inability to locate Dr. Cothran's office.

A choir of laughter fills the office. Over the din of giggles, the bespectacled one snorts, "Yes, you just may be. Did you take a wrong exit off the freeway?"

Embarrassed by their misinterpretation of my naïve but honest answer, I blush uncontrollably. "No, no, nothing like that. I'm looking for Dr. Cothran's office."

All typing has now ceased. I fear they can hear me sucking in deep breaths of air as I try to regain some composure.

"Dr. Cothran's office is in Harkness Hall in the School of Arts and Science Building next door," she nods her head to her right and rolls her eyes in the same direction. "He won't be in until Monday, though. His secretary will be here at eight, but don't expect him until about nine or ten. His office is on the second floor."

"Thank you," I swallow the ma'am, a token of respect I normally reserve for older women. Then in a befuddled acknowledgment of the others now staring intently, I turn to retreat and repeat, "Thank you, ma'am."

"Say, are you one of Dr. Cothran's incoming students?"

"Yes," I assert a little more boldly than necessary.

"We heard we were gonna get some of y'all." The female conductor signals for another round of giggles.

I wheel around and make it for fresh air. The light-headedness and dizziness that had gripped me for most of the morning has lifted. I begin to understand my unique situation and try to convince myself that this will be an experience of a lifetime and one I will never forget. Thinking to myself, I will soon learn how a Negro must feel when he walks among whites. I enter into a contract with myself, when I answer in the affirmative to the query as to whether I am going to be a student—here at Atlanta University. They may carry me out of here but I swear to myself, I will not let anything deny me the education I came to get.

September 14, 1967

Dear Lorreta,

Well, are you ready for a shock? Atlanta University has no undergrads...it is strictly a graduate level school. It also is an all colored grad school. Because the money for my fellowship came from federal funds, I was chosen by a board outside the school. To my knowledge, I am the only white person on campus – 1600 people on campus.

When I finally got back to the Atlantan after I discovered this shocking news, I flopped on my bed and just stared at the walls. There and then I decided when and if I get out of here, I am going to get as far north and as far west as I can. These people down here make me 'nervous.'

Lorreta – (I bet I'm spelling your name wrong) anyway Lorreta, every time I think of you, and that is almost perpetual, I get a funny feeling. I am hungry to see you again…

I hope you are not afraid that this place will change me. It will only make me feel stronger towards you and everything you stand for. If ever given the chance, I will do all within my power to protect you from things that I experienced today.

I love you –
Duane

3

The Dorm Room

On Monday at 8:45 a.m., I return to my hotel after having the greasiest egg omelet and soggiest toast ever when I spot a parked taxi with a colored driver. This will make my getting to Atlanta University easier, I surmise as I walk up to the open cab window. "I've got business at Atlanta University Administrative Offices. Can you get me there?"

"Yes, suh," the driver gives me a thorough going over but says no more. He takes a different route and I'm concerned that the taxi driver is taking me to Georgia Tech but then we cross the railroad overpass. I sit quietly. I don't initiate any conversation that might expose my recent arrival in this new world. I then recognize what looks like a huge graystone church just a block before the driver takes a left. I look and note the street name is Chestnut. I've only been here once but it already feels familiar. While I have no specific appointment time set with Dr. Cothran, I experience a sense of expectation. I know where I am going. My heart's still racing and my temples are pulsing but this time it's not from the unknown but from a wonderment of what the brick and mortar of this institution of higher education holds for me.

"That will be $2, suh," I thrust all three singles crumpled in my sweaty palm and step out onto the curb. The driver leans over and with a bit of surprise, politely says, "Well, thank you suh. Y'all have a nice day."

"You too," I venture and wheel around and start toward the School of Arts and Science Building. Inside, I reach the second floor and begin down a corridor with closed wooden doorways on both sides. It could easily be a clinic or hospital as each door nameplate has this *Dr.* or that *Dr.*'s name stenciled in black enamel. I come across an open doorway and stick my neck in to see if this cell belongs to Dr. Cothran.

There it is—in bold letters declaring DR. COTHRAN/CHAIRMAN. It immediately strikes me that this office belongs to someone of prestige, not just another faculty *Dr.* of some anonymous academic discipline. This is the headquarters of the man that rules over all the fiefdoms found in this institution of higher learning. Simultaneously with a rush of anxiety, as if I just stepped through the ropes of a boxing ring, I realize the office holds two occupants. One is a light-skinned woman in her mid-twenties standing at a desk bent over an open drawer. The bushy style of her reddish-brown hair engulfs her face like a halo. Light blue eye shadow softens the piercing sharpness of her dark brown eyes. A bit of rouge accents her cheeks making them appear higher and more pronounced. Her lips are painted an orange-red that somehow complements her beauty but doesn't fit in with the stuffy surroundings. Her silky gold blouse is tucked into a gold chain belt that adorns a skirt wrapped about overstated buttocks that betray too many hours spent sitting.

Hardly noticeable in the shadow of this radiant woman's splendor sits the second occupant, a tall thin man maybe a year or two my junior. He's perched on a pew-like bench of darkened oak. He wears a red, white, and blue-striped terry-cloth T-shirt with gray dress slacks. He looks up from the book cradled in his lap and quickly places his large black and white running shoes on the floor. A sparsely whiskered Vandyke and mustache encircles a pensive, narrow-lipped mouth. He reaches and strokes his pittance of a beard looking from me to the woman who is still busy looking through the contents of the drawer. A studied look of bewildered annoyance crosses his face, as if he suddenly determines the source of an unwanted interruption. I nod a silent greeting but know it isn't going to be returned.

A growing awkward silence is interrupted by the jangle of the telephone in the middle of the secretary desk that dominates the room. The woman reaches to answer it with one hand while half-waving, half-signaling— "You're next."

"Good morning, Dr. Cothran," her words hold a sweet and throaty alto tone. "Well yes, a Mr. Burton is here to see you and I do believe one of your fellowship people just walked in." After a short pause, she covers the mouthpiece and looking directly at me, she asks, "What did you say your name was?"

"Duane Johnson," I answer knowing this is not the time or place to be cute by pointing out that I haven't given my name.

"It's Mr. Wayne Johnson. Yes, I will post a notice and tell anyone who drops by. Well, have a nice day and we'll see you tomorrow," she says and depresses the receiver before placing the business end of the telephone in its resting position. She stands as if she is about to address a larger audience than she has and says, looking solely at the other person in the room, "Dr. Cothran is tied up off campus and won't be in today. He says the two of you should see Mrs. Green in Admissions and get settled in your dorm. Should read He doesn't want to see any students before the department meeting tomorrow at nine. It'll be in the end classroom on this floor. He'll answer all your questions and introduce everyone to the faculty. He knows about your situation, Mr. Burton, and says not to be concerned."

"I was to notify Dr. Cothran of my acceptance of the fellowship and I haven't done that yet. Do you know if there's anything else I need to do?" I ask.

"Well, you're here aren't you? We took all the 'no' responses as positives," she blurts with a short laugh and looks to Mr. Burton to see if he caught her humor. "As far as I know, five out of ten have declined and one has sent a written notice of acceptance. So, no matter what, you'll have company. But y'all had best get down and get yourselves a dorm room. We are going to be running shorter than usual with all the folks we're taking in this year."

"And where do we do that?" I ask politely.

"Go to the first floor of the Admissions Office and ask for Mrs. Green. She's expecting y'all. She will get you registered and give you a room number in Ware Hall. Y'all can move in today. Some already moved in over the weekend."

"That's what I need to see the Dr. about—uh, to see if I can get some, uh, financial assistance with school," Mr. Burton quietly announces in a questioning tone.

"Well, Dr. Cothran says he knows about your situation and for you not to be concerned. I don't know, but you'll probably get one of the OEO fellowships. I wrote a letter for the doctor asking for clearance to reassign the fellowships to students already in the program. I'd get me a dorm room and get to the department meeting tomorrow and go with the flow until someone says uh-uh. *Stake your flag*, my mama always told me," advises the secretary.

Learning more about my situation, I thank Dr. Cothran's secretary for her help and turn and retreat slowly down the hall. I can hear Mr. Burton's shuffling footsteps behind me. I deliberately slow down to let him catch up. I want company in my efforts to find my way around and he is the only fellow student I have met. When I reach the top of the stairs and he has yet to come alongside me, I stop and wait until he's within arm's reach. I stick out my hand and say, "I'm Dooane Johnson. Please call me Dooane. It looks like we're heading to the same place. Do you mind some company, Mr. Burton?"

"Uh, ah actually, no—that's cool. Yeah, I guess you're going to see Mrs. Green. You can call me Lonnie," he utters with all the pleasure of someone that has been asked to do some unpleasant task.

"Where you from?" I ask as we descend the stairs.

"Cleveland. You from Texas?"

"No. Montana," *this guy is not trying very hard I think to myself. No Montanan wants to be mistaken for being a Texan, especially on an all-black campus in Atlanta, Georgia.*

An uneasy silence arises as I lead the way to the office I visited on Saturday.

"This Mrs. Green's office?" Lonnie asks.

"I don't know, but I know this is the Admissions Office. There will be someone here who can direct us."

Together, we step through the double-door entrance and I recognize some of the same women from Saturday. Again, everyone appears preoccupied with the task at hand.

I announce to no one in particular, "We were sent to see Mrs. Green."

The closest typist points a long, chocolate brown arm and index finger to our left. Obediently, we turn to see a cashier-like window into a smaller room immediately adjacent to this typist bullpen. I get to the window one step ahead of Mr. Burton and stick my head inside and inquire of the only occupant, "Mrs. Green?"

"Yes," the middle-aged woman slowly drawls, and then looks up and seeing me, she straightens in her desk chair. "Yes, I'm Mrs. Green. How may I help you?" Before she finishes her polite acknowledgment, she stands and busily comes to the window.

"We were sent here by Dr. Cothran's assistant to get our dorm room assignments," I try to sound official but polite.

"Y'all fellowship people?"

Her inquiring look seems to be directed at me, so I answer, "Yes, I'm Duane Johnson and this is ..."

"Lonnie Burton," he finishes with a definite ring of *I can answer for myself* in my newly found associate's intonation.

"Let me get my list." Mrs. Green picks a clipboard from her desk that has several sheets of typewriter-size paper clipped to it, "I don't see Burton here—but Johnson is in Room 238."

"What's the significance if you're not on that list?" Lonnie asks, sounding more offended than concerned.

"Well, the fellowship people are assigned to single-occupancy rooms, and they are all taken. But I'll tell you what we'll do for the time being. Mr. Stone has notified us that he and his family will be living off campus for the fall semester—at least. I will assign his room to you and if he decides to move back on campus next semester, he will have to take whatever is vacant. How's that?" Mrs. Green smiles politely looking pleased that she's solved another room assignment problem so quickly.

Lonnie provides no response.

"Did you want a roommate?" asks Mrs. Green in an attempt to understand his hesitancy.

"No … no, the single room is cool. I am just wondering if I should check with Dr. Cothran before, you know, I uh, take someone else's room."

"Well, Dr. Cothran will send you right back to me and I'll warn you the unclaimed rooms are assigned on a first-come basis. We're just not going to have enough room at Ware Hall this year. If the room doesn't meet your needs you can give it up. There will be plenty of takers this year." Mrs. Green doesn't come across as impatient but more with of a sense of confidence. And then as if she is sure her maternal-like counsel is sufficiently persuasive, she adds, "You'll be in Room 237. Housekeeping will give you the keys. Make sure you report any damage before you move in. Class enrollment packets will be available after one o'clock tomorrow."

"Thank you, ma'am," Lonnie's quiet gratitude is hardly audible. And just as quietly, he asks, "And how does one find Ware Hall from here?"

"Go to the front of this building and you'll be on Chestnut. Take a left and walk two-and-a-half blocks. It'll be across the street on your right. If you come to Hunter Street, you've gone too far. If you mistake Bumstead Hall, the female dorm for y'all's dorm, they will correct you. It's not difficult. You'll find it easy. Are you driving?"

"No," is my quick response.

"Yes, I have a car," Lonnie's response had a "What now?" ring to it.

"Parking is a premium. You'll have to park on the street wherever you can find a place but be careful not to park in someone's driveway. The university wants to be a good neighbor," Mrs. Green raises her voice slightly as if everyone including the two graduate students should pay heed to her advice.

As we leave the building, Lonnie and I are greeted by a furnace-like blast of hot muggy air. While Harkness Hall is not air-conditioned, its interior marbled hallways are shaded by huge deciduous trees. Now outside the building and out from under the shade, Atlanta's late summer mid-morning sun is punishing.

"Holy shit, it gets hot down here. You could fry an egg on the sidewalk," I say, again feeling like I'm walking into a steam bath.

"I think July and August are the hottest months," Lonnie seems reassuring in his first unsolicited exchange. "I've seen it plenty hot in Cleveland but not this humid. But the winters are much nicer here."

We continue left without any further conversation. When we reach the corner, we see several student types hanging around in front of a wooden frame building kitty-corner to the campus. Lonnie offers, "That's the bookstore. They also sell sandwiches and cold drinks."

"Are you hungry? How about something to drink?"

Lonnie crosses the street and keeps walking toward Ware Hall as if he's by himself. I know that he probably feels uncomfortable being seen with me. Halfway through the next block, Lonnie looks up and down the street and motions for us to cross to the shady side. Then as an overdue afterthought, Lonnie says, "I think the prices are inflated in the bookstore. Probably because they think they have a monopoly. I haven't bought anything there and I don't intend to."

"How you gonna get your textbooks if that's the university bookstore?" I don't know if Lonnie is being candid or if he feels he needs a reason for not venturing closer to the bookstore with me in tow.

"I'll find used books or borrow them. I'm not going to give a monopoly any more business than I have to. I'm not too sure that the store is not owned by the Man."

Who *the Man* Lonnie is shunning is unknown to me? I think about asking but don't want to appear ignorant; there will probably be another chance to get filled in.

It turns out that Bumstead Hall is connected to Ware Hall by the dining room. The entrance to Bumstead is adorned with a wide circular brick-paved driveway and a much more ornate entrance. Flowering bushes and huge magnolia trees give the entryway the opulence of a large estate. Less affluent in appearance is the entrance to the men's dorm Ware Hall.

My breath hitches as we enter and shut the door, there's an overwhelming stench of lye and paint. A short, rotund woman in her late forties is standing behind an enclosed receptionist area. "Miss Clara will be here in a minute. She the head housekeeper, you wanna talk to her," was her nice but *don't ask me* greeting.

The interior of the red brick dorm is light green-painted stucco adorned with dark mahogany woodwork. I notice a long, dark hallway to our right. I take a couple of steps and look closer at a brass sign with an arrow and DINING ROOM inscribed on it. Our greeter warns me, "The painters haven't finished the recreation room and the dining room doesn't open until tomorrow."

"Oh, okay! Thanks," I return to stand alongside of Lonnie. In the meantime, two young black college students enter the dorm from the street and stare quizzically at Lonnie and me before hurrying down a hallway to the left. I hear them muttering something about a "honky-tonk" or maybe it is a "honky and a Tom." I don't follow which individual is making the hushed growling.

A large, espresso colored man decked out in white painter coveralls comes down the steps and opens the front door; he places a wooden wedge at the bottom of the door to keep it open. "We gotta keep these doors open while we're painting or we gonna suffocate."

"Miss Clara said to keep the doors closed," the receptionist declares defensively.

"You tell Miss Clara I say to keep the doors open if she wants us to finish the painting," the big man asserts, his deep voice resonates throughout the entranceway. He shakes his head at Lonnie and me as he disappears down the hallway toward the dining room.

"Several long, quiet minutes pass before a trim woman with dark brown hair in a net, wearing a green dress that closely matches the color of the dorm walls descends the stairs, carrying a clipboard and a pair of green rubber gloves. Something about her reminds me of my own mother; it may be her petite build or brisk movements.

"Miss Clara, the painters opened the door, I told them you wanted them shut, and these boys have been waiting to see you," the elderly receptionist shares her sense of priorities.

"That's okay, Miss Ida. Leave them open. They been complaining they need more air." Then turning to Lonnie and me, Miss Clara explains, "I try to keep the doors closed during the midday heat. That way it keeps cooler in here. But I understand what the painters are saying. I guess hot air is better'n no air. How can I help you two gentlemen?"

After a moment of hesitation, I speak in an effort to fill the silent void, "Mrs. Green sent us to get the keys and move into 237 and 238."

"Hmm! Let me see. I think those rooms have been painted but I don't believe the housekeepers have had a chance to tidy up and make the beds." Looking down a list of hand-printed notes on her clipboard, Miss Clara nods and says, "I can let you sign out the keys now but you won't be able to move in until after 3:00 p.m.—maybe not until tomorrow. Also, the painters haven't gotten to that hallway. But if you don't clutter up the hallways, I'll let you move in for sure tomorrow."

"Sounds okay with me," I respond, careful not to suggest that I'm talking for Lonnie, growing more aware of his desire to be recognized as someone who can exercise his own independence and not allow anyone, especially a white male, to speak for him.

"Mm-hmm, how about letting us take a look at the rooms before we move in?" Lonnie surprises me a little with his assertiveness.

"Well, sure. All I ask is that you stay off the second floor until after 3:00 p.m. so as to let the painters and housekeeping finish their work up there." Now I know what it is about Miss Clara that reminds me of my mother; she takes charge of every situation and has her way of letting you know who is in charge.

Sept. 17, 1967

Hi Lorreta,

Howdy! Today, I made arrangements to move into the men's dorm. I will have a private room. The last one available too! I paid registration fees and met Dr. Cothran's Administrative Assistant. He is the man who sent me the telegram notifying me of my fellowship.

My room number in Ware Hall is 238. I don't know if I will get a box number or if I will receive mail at the dorm. The dorm houses the grad students only so it should be a little different from regular college dorm life – of which I know little of. My room seems very clean. We have meals cafeteria style and we pay for the meals as we receive them. They start feeding tomorrow so will keep my fingers crossed until I find out how the chow is.

I met a young man (colored) from Cleveland who stuck with me and showed me the ropes. He took me into the colored ghetto located close to Ware Hall – Kid, I have never experienced anything like it! I was confronted with many hate stares. Not really stares – but when I would catch somebody just noticing me, I would observe a deepening of the brows and even an occasional sneer. My friend and I had one bad experience. We were walking by a pool hall when one Negro stepped out and bummed a cigarette off of me. I gave him a cig and then he wanted money. I said, "Sorry fella, I'm broke." He became real nasty and tried to block the sidewalk when we attempted to walk away. We outmaneuvered him and got the 'hell' out of there. The rest of the afternoon Lonnie (my friend) apologized. We finally laughed it off. But I don't mind admitting…I lost my cools. I finally told Lonnie that I had to take a shower and went back to my hotel.

Students were moving in by the hundreds yesterday. There are many foreign students from all parts of the world plus many Negro students and then me. I am very anxious to register and begin classes. The social life here for me looks very dim, especially being without a car. But I didn't come here for a fabulous social life and I only hope that nothing will distract me from my studies. I am still in doubt about what particular courses I will take and how my schedule will be.

I will forward my mailing address to you as soon as I know it. I hope you will find time to write me and keep me informed on the haps back in good old Montana.

I looked at the calendar and found that Christmas vacation begins December 16th and ends January 3rd. I think I will make plane reservations about October 1st so that I will be sure to get home over the holidays. Finals for the first semester are at the end of January. I might be home for good then.

Sweet Pea, you would be really proud of me. I have lost pounds plus. Since I got here, I have been walking three to five hours and only eating two meals a day. None of my clothes fit me. I must be down to 135 anyway – would you believe 155.

I miss Montana and you very much. I hope you are doing a bang-up job student teaching. I know you are anxious to get back to Bozeman – the home of those big bad Bobcats. I can hardly wait until next June. Kid, I'm thinking faster than I can write so I hope you can fill in wherever I seem to wander. I don't want to bother you with a mess of mush but I do want to remind you...that's remind you...that I still do!

I am going to see if they offer a course in letter writing so I can improve my narrative ability. It must be very dull reading my accounts of a grad student. Oh well, I fill up the page. See ya in my dreams.

Bye for now,
Duane

4

Crossing Over The Bridge Of Demarcation

I wait for Lonnie outside on the porch. The air is not a lot cooler but it isn't laden with the paint and lye smell that fills the dorm hallways. Pocketing his room key and receipt in his back pocket, Lonnie nearly walks by before I engage him, "Whatcha got planned for the next half-hour?"

Looking at me blankly, Lonnie is slow to answer, "Not much I guess."

"I'll give you five bucks to take me by my hotel and pick up my stuff. If we can get it before noon, I'll buy us something to eat."

"My car's pretty small. What all you got?"

"Two suitcases and a typewriter," I begin to calculate whether it might be less costly to call a cab. I don't want Lonnie to think he's encountered some kind of leach that will take some extraordinary effort to get rid of.

"Well okay. My car is cluttered with some of my stuff. But if your stuff will fit and you help me get my stuff moved in, I'll do it. Wait here and I'll go get my car."

"I'll go with ya." I didn't want the guy to distance himself and decide to dog me. I need to be checked out of the hotel before noon or I'll get stuck paying for another day.

"No, you stay here. My car is parked at some friends. I don't know how they will take to you." Lonnie's matter of fact tone has a definite *take it or leave it* ring to it.

"All right, I was just trying to save us some time. I need to get out of my room by noon." I agree half-understanding that I might pose a liability to Lonnie in this part of town.

Managing to get to the Atlantan Hotel and sparing any additional charges, I check out before noon. I move three bags of books to the floor and place my two suitcases, which barely fit, onto the back seat of Lonnie's Volkswagen Bug. I elect to cradle my typewriter on my lap, fearing damage to the electric contraption.

"Let's get some chow." I smile, relieved that everything fits and knowing we still have a couple of hours before we can claim possession of our rooms at Ware Hall.

"Not in this part of town," Lonnie's discomfort shows on his brow.

We have trouble finding our way back to the railroad overpass, neither of us realizing the spoke-like grid street layout in downtown Atlanta. The black bug finally sputters up the arch of the tallest bridge crossing dry land that I've ever seen. "I wonder what this bridge is called?" I ask peering out the window I see more railroad tracks below than can be counted from my vantage point.

"I don't know, but they ought to call it the *Bridge of Demarcation*," Lonnie answers with a sideway look to see if I understand.

I didn't, "Why?"

"If you haven't noticed, everything on the north side of the bridge is white, everything on the south side is black. And they put all those railroad tracks down there so that the only way back and forth is across this bridge. These Atlanta Whites are pretty sly." Lonnie's assertion is matter of fact and doesn't betray the bitterness I will soon face.

"Yeah, I guess I see what you mean."

The vibration of the bug as it is propelled along by its sputtering and underpowered engine is all that fills a noisome quiet as we drive south on Highway 20. Blocks turn into miles. I can see huge airplanes taking off and landing in the skyline ahead of us.

"Let's pull into that McDonald's up ahead," I suggest, nodding toward the Golden Arches. Both of my hands are holding the increasingly heavy typewriter.

"You think this neighborhood looks okay?" Lonnie asks in all seriousness.

Before making any real assessment, I blurt, "Yeah, why not? Besides, I need a break from this damn typewriter." We park and get out. I'm about a half-dozen steps from the car when I realize Lonnie hasn't joined me. Not sure why he isn't jumping at the chance to get out of the oven-like oil can-smelling bug, I turn and ask, "Why don't you come with me and order whatever you want?"

"Na, I don't eat red meat and I doubt if they have anything I can eat. Go ahead and get yourself something."

"Hey, we made a deal. I'd buy lunch if we got out of my hotel before noon. If this isn't good enough for you, just say so. We can go someplace else."

Without commenting further, Lonnie slowly rolls up the windows, gets out and locks the driver's door, and with a scornful look he saunters alongside me as I approach the chest-high order window. A neatly groomed teenage girl with a blonde ponytail and long, black eyelashes asks without looking up, "Your order please!"

"I'll have a Big Mac, a large order of fries, and a large Coke," it's my standard order.

Lonnie stands squinting at the menu displayed above the order window, "What kind of fish comes in the Filet-O-Fish?"

"Perch, I think," drawls the young order taker, as she looks up from the register with an amused glare.

"Is the fish cooked kosher?" Lonnie inquires.

"It's deep-fried and comes on a bun with our own tartar sauce, or you can have ketchup." I don't think the young lady knew what "kosher" meant. I know I didn't. He ponders the menu and the response to his question long enough for me to begin to feel embarrassed, Lonnie painstakingly recites his order. "I would like the Filet-O-Fish with tartar on the side, a small order of fries, and a small lemonade, please."

I pay and join Lonnie at one of a half-dozen metal tables under the shade trees. A white couple in their mid-thirties sit down three tables away and openly leer at the sight of Lonnie and me. A woman with three children ranging in ages from four to seven cautions her children, "Don't stare at strangers." She fails, however, to heed her own advice.

When our order number is called, I motion for Lonnie to stay put while I retrieve our meals. While I'm still somewhat naïve about race relations in the South, there is little doubt that those who are present are scowling their disapproval of a white person seating himself at the same table as a black. I feel uncomfortable. I don't know any of these people but still feel embarrassed at their visible condemnation. In between a bite of burger and a French fry, I ask Lonnie, "Why don't you eat meat, man?"

"I eat some meat but not anything that has pig in it, like in **hamburger**. It's in accord with my religion."

"You Jewish?" I ask showing more surprise than I mean to.

"No. I recently converted to the Muslim faith. We don't believe in ingesting anything unclean."

"What makes pigs unclean?"

"It goes back many centuries in sacred writings. Even the White Man's Bible acknowledges that pigs are unclean. I think it's that they eat slop and live in food garbage."

"I know Jews don't eat pork, but I've never really understood why. I can buy the 'unclean' theory. What were you before you converted?"

"Methodist."

"How come you converted?"

Lonnie studies me for some time before answering, "Because I believe Christianity is a white man's religion and it's used to keep the black man down. The Southern plantation owners forced their religion on us when we were slaves. Their Bible supports the institution of slavery and justifies abusing us because of the color of our skin."

"I guess I've read something about that. Not all Christians nor all whites believe slavery was right."

"Then why is the Man still enslaving the black man in ghettos, keeping him in pay-nothing jobs, and trying to prevent him from voting? Why is it that black men make up only 10 percent of the population but more than 80 percent of those in penitentiaries are black? Why does *whitey* turn their head and pretend not to see the exploitation of colored women and children?"

"I never thought about it like that before. But you can't overgeneralize and say all whites or all Christians are that way. There are a lot of colored Christians you know?" I don't want to get into a knockdown drag out argument with this guy but I also don't want him to think that I'm some sort of a wimp that won't stand up for the truth.

That's because they continue to be duped and doped by *the Man*. But there's a wake-up call being shouted by the brothers and sisters."

"Who is this *Man* that you're talking about?" I wonder if he's referring to President Johnson, and am about to inventory all that he and President Kennedy have done to end segregation and improve the fate of colored Americans.

"What? You're getting ready to go to Atlanta U and pursue graduate studies in sociology and you don't know who *the Man* is? You are either dumb or acting dumb."

"Well help me out. I really don't know."

"The brothers refer to the white man and all his institutions, his history, his schools, and his laws collectively as *the Man*. Have you never read Malcolm X? Have you white folks in Montana never heard of Stokely Carmichael? You know ignorance is just another form of exploitation?" The volume of Lonnie's vociferous rap is becoming louder and louder.

"Well, that's why I came to Atlanta U, to learn. I guess I have more to learn than I thought." I'd never heard of Malcolm X. I think Carmichael was the guy that purged (SNCC) the Student Nonviolent Coordinating Committee of whites. I don't understand his motives but reading about it did rub me the wrong way. Fearing the unveiling of my ignorance and feeling a bit at risk with my belongings in Lonnie's car, I humbly end the conversation.

On our way to Ware Hall, I venture asking Lonnie, "Did you see the looks we got back there? Man, if looks could kill!"

"Damned crackers! They probably think we're Freedom Riders. I don't think they've seen many whites and colored together, especially breaking bread with one another. I bet they didn't like me talking to you the way I did. Not polite for a nigger to talk down to a white. Damned racists— we're lucky they didn't call the sheriff on us. We could have been lynched."

The long silence that follows is anything but serene. Suddenly thoughts doubting the worth of continuing my education amid such a confused and hostile setting run through my mind. I decide that I won't be intimidated by my ignorance. I'm not going to let that old need to feel accepted and desire to be 'liked' interfere with my opportunity to get a master's degree. I sense that much of the education I'll receive here will be outside of the classroom. Besides I don't want to jump the gun and take it for granted that Lonnie's attitude toward whites is representative of all the colored students. But from deep inside I'm feeling vibes that are warning me not to be caught off guard or surprised.

As we drive toward Ware Hall, I am overwhelmed with mixed thoughts and emotions. On the one hand, I intellectually want to deny my own prejudices and denounce all of the hurt caused by the social apartheid that has existed in America for too long. On the other hand, I feel threatened by blacks, especially black men. There are many things that I hold dear, which I don't want to share with people who are different from me. And from my point of view, there is no greater difference than that which exists between black and white. I bite my tongue I recall the warnings of sage whites: *Give a nigger an inch and he'll take a mile. All them niggers want is to have a white woman. Maybe the Ku Klux Klan was right to fight for keeping colored people 'in their place.'* Wasn't it a clergyman or politician from Mississippi who said, "If you don't keep the nigger in his place, he'll take your place, your job, your house, your wife?" I shudder realizing that I really don't know what I believe. Well, I'm going to keep my thoughts and questions to myself. I come to the realization that Lonnie's lamented fear about being lynched is not an overstated psychotic fear. It feels like I'm at the center of a huge social whirlpool of change and I'm not quite sure if I will survive it. There is a little voice inside me screeching, *"Run, run, run. No, I am not going to run. No, I am not going to quit. No! No! No!*

"Whatcha say?" Lonnie looks at me.

"Nothing, I didn't say nothing."

* * *

While sitting at the carrel-like desk in my dorm room, I survey my surroundings. The room measures about 12 by 10 feet. Behind the door is a closet roomy enough for what are my clothes. The single bed looks like it belongs in an army barracks with its tightly made white sheets and a single olive-brown wool blanket. The pillow is encased in stark, white cotton that's about as thick as my *Webster's Seventh New Collegiate Dictionary*. I'm grateful for the window with a view of a huge tree the likes of which I never saw in Montana. I don't mind that I can't see beyond the foliage of the shady timber as I realize it will keep the morning sunlight from entering my room, hopefully keeping it cool longer. The walls and ceiling are a freshly painted pale green. The smell of the just-dried paint dominates. I appraise my half-dozen texts stored on a shelf above my typewriter. All are from classes I took at the College of Great Falls. I placed them in alphabetical order by author's last name. This is done solely from my desire for order. I know the books well and can differentiate one from the other by the color of the jacket. On the far left is John Dewey's *Human Nature and Conduct* alongside it is a scarcely read copy of *Social Change* edited by Amitai Etzioni and Eva Etzioni. The professor at the College of Great Falls had lectured extensively from other sources and everyone knew that memorizing class notes was all we needed to pass the midterm and final exams. Likewise, *The Nature and Types of Sociological Theory* by Don Martindale is one of the more labor-some texts I've experienced. I smile as my attention swings to the right of the short continuum as *Images of Man* by Mills, and Sorokin's *Contemporary Sociological Theories* complete my small collection of sociological wisdom. There are more stored at my folks' place but I didn't want the burden of carrying heavier suitcases. Worrisome thoughts cross my mind, as I fear failure because I don't have that knowledge at hand in some text that's packed away more than a thousand miles distant. I'm rescued from lapsing into parasitic anxiety by a soft knock at the door. "Who is it?" I am momentarily in a state of paranoia as a result of the culture shock I've experienced during the last couple of days.

"Lonnie Burton."

I swing open the door happy it's someone I know and relieved to be liberated from my little world of worry.

"You said you would help me with my stuff. I have a footlocker I need help with." Lonnie is soaked in perspiration from moving into the dorm. After he helped me with my suitcases, he had disappeared. I guessed he wanted some distance from me after spending the better part of the day answering my endless barrage of questions.

"No problem, man. Where's it at?"

"In my car parked out front."

Out front turned out to be half a block away—Lonnie has wrestled the wooden trunk from the back seat of his car onto the street. We each grab the handgrips on the ends of the two-by-four-foot receptacle and lift. We only manage to move it about fifty feet before we set the trunk down and rest.

"What the hell you got in here—bricks?"

"Just some books I brought from Cleveland. I moved everything else myself but you can see why I need your help with this."

I'm not sure if Lonnie is bragging about his independence or apologizing for cashing in on my promise from earlier that day. We are both dripping with perspiration in protest to the sweltering heat and the strain of getting the trunk into the dorm. Staggering down the second-floor hallway, we both silently acknowledge that one more respite is necessary. Lonnie sits, resting on the trunk as I lean against the wall.

Just as we're about to make another, hopefully final, effort to get the locker to its new home a tall, slender, young-looking coffee-colored man approaches us. He looks just as burdened down as we are. When he's about thirty feet from us, his eyes widen as if he's seen a ghost. With a shrill scream, he drops his trunk and turns running back the way he had come.

"What was that all about?" I am dumbfounded. Guessing the basis for the bizarre act, I probe further, "Was he putting us on? What in the hell was his problem?"

Lonnie breaks into an uncontrolled chuckle. "Oh my! I don't think he expected to see a honky in his new home. If the brother was acting, he sure enough is good at it. No, I think he must be one of those that's never gone to a school with whites. You sure enough got his attention."

"Let's get this trunk into your room before we start a riot," I am only half-kidding.

"You are a riot. It will be worth the price of admission to see you walk across campus tomorrow."

We both laugh so hard that we have to take another break to move the locker the remaining short distance. Lonnie's room is right across from mine. I leave him to unload his books and return to my abode.

September 18, 1967

Dear Folks,

Well, I have moved into the dorm here at Atlanta University! I have a single room on the second floor of a dorm that must house about 500 male students. There is a mixture of foreign students who come from all parts of the world and American Negroes and me. The fellow across the hall is a colored guy from Cleveland, Ohio. He has been very good in showing me around and educating me insofar as what or how a white man is expected to act in a Negro community.

Living here is an experience of a lifetime. I often wondered how a Negro felt as he walked among whites, knowing that he stuck out as an oddity. You become very aware of the way people look at you and talk to you. The 'hate stare' is a reality that sends you to bed at night feeling very alone. I hope that when classes start, I will be too busy to notice too much of this. Most of all, I hope nothing will interrupt my studies.

I am a little homesick right now. The lack of something constructive to do is a contributing thing. It will do me good to be without a car for a while. Although my social life would be a lot different, but then, I didn't come here for social life.

I haven't sent home any money as yet. I have about $300 left but I do not know how much I will need before my money from the fellowship is straightened out. I found out that we will pay for the meals that we eat as we eat them. I do not know what the cost will be. I have lost a little weight since I came here but it has been from walking around for three to five hours a day.

The weather here is unbelievable at this time. I do not know what the highs are but it is really balmy but not to the point of being uncomfortable.

Well, I'll call it a day now! Things are A-OK here. I'll keep you informed on the haps. And I'll practice my typing a bit before writing again.

Love you all,
Duane

P.S. I don't have a post office box number yet so hold out from writing until I tell you my right address.

My College of Great Falls senior photo

My mother and I leave for my graduation ceremony.

Enjoying my 1967 Corvette before I leave for Atlanta

Summer of 1967 I meet and fall in love with Loretta

Loretta falsely believes I am rich

5

The Welcome

I awaken at 6:00 a.m. and I'm the only person in the shower facilities. It's convenient that the bathroom is next to my room. This way, I can dart to and from showering, shaving, and using the bathroom without dressing. Across the hall is Lonnie's room. There's a tomblike silence in the dorm at this time of day. The dining room is open from 7:00 a.m. to 8:30 a.m. for breakfast.

At precisely 7:00 a.m., I knock on Lonnie's door. Getting no answer, I knock again, this time with a heavier hand. Moments later, Lonnie opens the door only enough to assess the early morning caller. He lets the door swing open and yawns and stretches, pulling a nylon sock from his head, he's attired in a pair of pajamas. It's obvious that my knocking woke him up. I'm taken aback as to why anyone would wear pajamas in Atlanta's early autumn heat and humidity but don't know Lonnie well enough to question his bedtime sleepwear.

"I'm headed down to the dining room. Want to join me for breakfast?"

Squinting at his wristwatch, Lonnie answers with a tired groan. "No. I don't eat breakfast."

"How about a cup of coffee then?"

"I don't drink coffee."

"Okay. How about going to Cothran's meeting together? I'll pick you up at 8:30."

"Why so early? We're less than ten minutes from his office."

"I like to arrive before the crowd and attract less attention," I explain

"Okay, how about 8:45?"

"That's cool."

The dining room which is locked except during designated meal periods, is located on the main floor of the three-story brick dormitory building. Bumstead Hall is the south wing while Ware Hall is the north wing.

A plump, smiling coal black woman in her early forties has just unlocked the men's entrance to the cafeteria-styled dining room when I arrive. I queue up behind nine or ten hushed students waiting ahead of me. The pleasant aroma of coffee and fried bacon wafts out the open door. I focus on the choices and posted prices and am not aware that there's no one lined up behind me. After loading my tray with tomato juice, toast, bacon, and coffee I approach the cash register attendant. Like the other four attendants, she is dressed in a neatly pressed powder-blue uniform. She places the change on my tray, ignoring my outreached hand and doesn't acknowledge my 'thank you.'

Once I sit down, I notice a long line of men and women students start to file through the cafeteria lineup. The hushed whispers give way to noisy chatter mixed with occasional squeals of laughter. The dining room is furnished with square tables dressed in white tablecloths. Each table has four chairs but some are moved to accommodate a fifth or sixth diner at another table. I am the sole diner at my table. A chair from my table is silently liberated by a bifocal-wearing Negro in a long-sleeved white shirt and blue dress pants.

The coffee is robust but lacks the customary bitter taste of a brew this strong. It is the best-tasting coffee I've had in a long time. I drain my cup and look around to see how the dishes are bussed. I catch a number of quizzical stares, which divert when our eyes meet. I decide to ask one of the attendants. I approach the woman that unlocked the door earlier. Her early morning smile gave me a sense of comfort.

"Leave them on the table, hon."

My thank you isn't acknowledged but I leave feeling like I just survived an important test. I walk briskly back to my room with my head held high. My watch reads 17 minutes to nine when I knock on Lonnie's door. My knuckles are still rapping when the door flies open. Lonnie looks freshly scrubbed; his beard and hair appear to be recently trimmed. Wearing a blue and yellow-striped pullover shirt with brown dress pants, he looks every part of a collegiate on the first day of school.

"I'm ready. Let's go."

Lonnie looks at the notebook and pen I'm carrying, and asks, "You think we're gonna need that?"

"Just in case."

"I haven't picked up all my stuff yet. Will you lend me a couple of sheets if we need to take notes?"

"No problem. Let's go. We don't want to be late and attract unnecessary attention, do we?"

We're surprised that the morning carries a brisk freshness when we were expecting it to be hot and muggy. It's one of those mornings that make you feel fortunate to be alive. We cross the street in front of Bumstead Hall to take advantage of the early sun. Lining the streets are single family homes. With one or two exceptions, the homes are neatly painted. Each is complemented by trimmed shrubs. Flowerbeds with a wide selection of roses, dahlias, and zinnias are neatly displayed in a number of yards. Most properties have hedges standing as privacy centurions. Several have wooden picket fences. Two ladies stand chatting on the sidewalk while leaning on yellow straw brooms to sweep the walkway clean.

"Good morning, ladies," I happily greet the two middle-aged neighbors.

"Morning," Their response is as one.

On the first block south of Ware Hall stands a gray wooden grocery store. Pasted on top of advertisements for cigarettes and soft drinks is a handmade sign, NO NEW CREDIT. The smell of vegetables and old meat greet us as we pass the open doorway. A thin woman dressed in shorts and a halter top exits the store smoking a cigarette and a pack of cigarettes in her hand.

"Good morning," I cheerfully say.

She looks a bit startled and then breaks into a broad toothless grin, "Morning!"

The sidewalks become more and more congested as we get closer to the main campus. Students who have been able to find parking on the street are scurrying to class. Lonnie and I walk in a less-hurried pace.

One resident with her hair tied up in a bandana and wearing a bright, red apron is setting fire to a pile of garbage piled on the street. I notice several other heaps smoldering in the gutter or on the streets along the way, adding a pungent odor to the air which overwhelms the freshness of the new morning. The presence of flattened tin cans bedecking the streets from gutter to gutter is explained. After exchanging heartfelt morning greetings and once we're out of earshot, I ask Lonnie, "Why do they do that?"

"Probably because the city doesn't pick up garbage in this part of town and it's too expensive to pay for private disposal. Burning it also keeps the rats from feasting," Lonnie continues.

"Bullshit—I can't believe a city this size doesn't have public garbage disposal."

"You never been to Cleveland, have you." It was a statement, not a question. "Duane, you sure enough are a country dude."

"What do ya mean?" I doubt his observation was meant as a complement.

"Well, a city dude wouldn't say good morning to everyone he sees. And if you live in a city you would know about the problem of getting rid of your garbage. Besides, them boots you're wearing give you away."

"Great Falls is a pretty big city. I just think it's polite to say hello to someone you make eye contact with."

"Only a country dude would make eye contact. How big is Great Falls?"

"About 50,000."

"That's the biggest city you lived in before coming here to Atlanta?"

"Yeah."

"Like I said, you a country dude. You better be careful not to let these city dudes shuck and jive you out of your beans."

There's standing room only by the time Lonnie and I make our way into the second-floor chamber. The room looks like a faculty lounge or some other sort of informal meeting place. The stale air in the mostly unused room gives way to a variety of perfumes, aftershave lotions, and soap. I don't try to count how many are there but have a sense of about 35 or so fellow students. Every size, shape, and shade of brown are present dressed in everything from suit and ties to bib overalls. Most of the women that seem to outnumber the men, wear summer print dresses. I notice that a couple of the women aren't wearing nylon stockings. The dominant dress for the men is short-sleeved shirts, looking as new as the school year, tucked into a variety of dress slacks. A few wear jeans. The group is an absolute contradiction to the conventional white slang that says, *all colored people look alike.*

As if by some magnetic force, my eyes lock on a white male first with a boot-camp crew cut. A short nod passes between us recognizing one's own kind. The second white male with long, blonde hair and a reddish complexion looks away when our eyes meet. He looks uncomfortable—I understand.

The chatter is cresting at a deafening level when a tall, sage-looking man in his early fifties walks through the door and approaches the podium staged in the middle of one end of the square room. His six-foot-plus height sets the frame for a proud-appearing athletic figure. Salt-and-pepper sideburns, wavy graying hair, and brown-rimmed glasses give the bicenturian a look of dignity. Dressed in a dark suit adorned with a blazing white shirt and rich red tie the man looks like a chief executive officer of some large corporation. He stands smiling while he waits for the prattle to turn to silence. Several students utter "shushes" until that's all that intrudes the now quiet room.

"Welcome to Atlanta University," he pauses and his grin turns to a wry smile. "I am Dr. Tillman C. Cothran, chair of the Department of Sociology and editor of *Phylon*. For those not yet acquainted with *Phylon*, it is the first and broadest read journal on race relations in the world."

He speaks with a slight British accent, maybe something he picked up in a previous academic position. His voice resonates in a rich, deep tone. His diction is precise. His cadence commands attention.

"You are the 102nd class to be invited to engage in the pursuit of higher learning at this fine institution." He shares more facts and history. I look around to see if anyone is taking notes. No one is but all are listening intently as Dr. Cothran's oration continues. My mind wanders but I'm jolted to attention when I hear something about white professors.

". . . While this may be new to some of you it is not new to Atlanta University. Since the opening of its doors Atlanta University has engaged White faculty to head classes attended by Negro scholars. And yes, many of their white offspring join in the pursuit of knowledge in classes matriculated by Negro scholars. The Sociology Department is happy to be accepting White candidates this year. For any of you that may be surprised let me assure you, we always have and always will accept White students. Even in the face of the wrath of the people of Georgia, Atlanta University stands firm. We unalterably endorse the co-education of the races here at Atlanta University as well as any other institution of education."

"Without regard to your complexion you will be expected to learn the basics that provide the framework for sociology and you will be expected to display such knowledge with the clarity historically identified with this department. This year we are accepting forty candidates to begin their studies with the start of this academic year. Twenty—only twenty—will be invited back to prepare themselves for admission to candidacy for a Masters of Arts. Whether all or none of these twenty become candidates for a graduate degree from this institution is solely dependent upon their academic performance," he pauses engaging in eye contact with each student. "In other words, we don't believe the normal curve should be used in setting academic standards. I need to remind you of certain facts. Atlanta University is proud of its standing as the Harvard of the South. To matriculate and to achieve the expected social status of an Atlanta University graduate you cannot be just as good as others with whom you will compete—you must be better than. Those of you who will be invited to pursue degrees must submit a thesis topic and research proposal by the midterm of the second semester. You will need to fashion a thesis committee made up of three faculty members. One, your advisor, a second faculty who will provide objective guidance, and myself." Grinning now more overtly than ever, he continues, "I will serve as chairperson on all thesis committees. In this manner I can assure adherence to our institution's standards. Any questions?"

One of the female students blurts out, "Where are these standards available?"

Poker-faced, Cothran responds, "You can become acquainted with them by signing up for one or more of my classes."

Several chuckles erupt but soon melt away under Cothran's unsmiling glare.

A couple of students breach the start of questions simultaneously.

In a gesture distinguishable as a professorial act, Cothran calls on an ink-black student dressed in a suit and tie.

"How come only twenty are asked to return for the second semester?"

Cradling his chin in one hand, Cothran softly shares the answer, "It has everything to do with resources and the desire to produce a few bright stars that will stand out in the community rather than a milky way that gets lost in the morning sunrise."

Students look at one another quizzically. An anonymous snort is all that follows.

Cothran nods at a fair-complexioned young woman who looks like she could model her tailored pink and blue suit. "What happens to those who don't come back?"

Bowing his head and shaking it in disbelief, Cothran laughingly says, "Oh, some of them go to other institutions of higher education; some of them graduate among the top of their class at such places as Howard, Berkeley, wherever. Some return home. We generally lose track of those."

"Are they allowed to start over in the next academic year?"

"No! What purpose would that serve?" Cothran looks again eye to eye with his captive audience.

"Have the Whites taken the place of brothers and sisters who may want to attend?" The question is too long for the heavyset male with a horrendous scar over his left eye to remain anonymous.

Cothran stares directly at the challenger, "What's your name?"

"Hector."

"Hector, help me understand the motivation of your question?"

Pausing, Hector says, "Well I am wondering if Whites count as part of the forty or whether, you know, uh, if they, uh, are over and above the forty?"

"There are only forty students invited to join us this semester," Cothran states as if the student should be able to figure out the answer for himself, not acknowledging the racial implications of the question. Not waiting for his response to sink in or lead to any sort of an exchange, Dr. Cothran points to another raised hand.

"I was looking at the catalog and I don't see a black studies major offered." The bespectacled student holds a copy of the catalog in his hand and stands with his mouth ajar waiting for a response.

"So, what is your question?" Dr. Cothran's tone hardens ever so slightly that many don't realize the question has hit a nerve with the professor.

"Well, you would think a Negro university would have a black studies program to prepare its Negro graduates to compete for teaching and administrative jobs that are springing up all over the country. This is 1967 you know." The mahogany-skinned student looks around the room to see if any others will support his supposition.

"You need to learn to pose your inquiries with much more clarity and succinctness if you wish to have serious thought given them. If you want to know why there are no courses or majors in black studies, let me say this: Many of the programs that are marketed under the guise of black studies are shallow responses to a momentary fad. If you are looking to be equipped for a particular job you might see in the current want ads, you have come to the wrong place. There are vocational tech schools galore that will eagerly enroll you. However, for those of you who wish to pursue knowledge that will endure the ebbing of such fads you will find adequate material to help you prepare to contribute to the broad arena of race relations. Let me briefly share the blueprint of our curriculum. We expect our students to dedicate one-third of their class work to the theoretical constructs that provide a platform for the study of sociology. At least another third of your time should be dedicated to acquiring the research tools that will assist you in assessing the relevancy or validity of various theses. Some of you may even find yourselves contributing to the framework of the discipline." Cothran bends at the waist, leaning toward his assembly and laughingly signals that he is having a bit of fun at our expense.

The gesture invites another brave challenge, "Is the curriculum here relevant to the 1960s? It sounds like Atlanta University is hung up with nineteenth-century material."

"Relevancy is a matter of appropriate timing and use of knowledge. We will provide you the knowledge but cannot dictate its use. We hope each

59

of you has come equipped with the necessary moral fiber and self-control to use this knowledge in a relevant fashion."

"What if you have questions regarding financial aid?" A bucktoothed coed looks directly at me as she spits out the question. I have a sudden feeling of guilt thinking everyone must know that I'm here on a full-ride fellowship.

"You should have answered those sorts of questions before coming here," Cothran says with slight annoyance, the meeting has gone on just about fifty minutes. I sense that was the last question. In a hushed tone, as if not wanting everyone to hear, Cothran adds, "Specific questions can be brought to me during my office hours." Then, louder he announces, "Class schedules and enrollment forms are available as you leave. Please have your enrollment cards filled out and signed by the designated faculty before classes begin on Thursday."

"Why do we start classes in the middle of the week?" The question is paid no heed. The meeting is over. Head held high, shoulders back, Cothran purposefully marches across the hall to his office. I see the two Whites from the meeting waiting for me at the top of the stairwell.

The dark-haired one speaks first, "Do you feel a little outnumbered?"

I don't bother to answer.

The taller blonde-haired guy suggests we go outside where there's more air. Once outside we exchange introductions. Bruce has crystal-clear blue eyes set close together over a narrow sharply wedged nose and chin. His hair is close to being black but appears lighter because of the closely cropped crew cut. He looks like he might be career military.

Forbes is taller than both Bruce and me. His dishwater blonde hair is long and it looks like it's been eight weeks since his last trim. Mind you, it's still not long enough to qualify him as a hippie. Behind clear, plastic-framed glasses his milky blue irises are set in reddened eyes. His pale, fleshy face is punctuated by full lips. Placing a filtered cigarette between his teeth he asks, "What do we have in common, besides obviously being white, that has placed us in this predicament?"

I roll my shoulders upward, a shrug acknowledging ignorance.

Bruce says, "I bet you two worked for OEO." He pulls a pipe out from his light, tan corduroy sports coat and lights it with the torch of a silver metal Zippo. Not receiving any argument, he continues, "Unless I'm terribly wrong, you are both recipients of fellowships created in honor of Sergeant Shriver, at the time he stepped down from running the Office of Economic Opportunity. It was his idea to help put pressure on Emory Medical School. Their trustees can no longer point at Atlanta University and claim a double standard. You know that Robert Kennedy was involved in trying to get Emory integrated?"

I have to admit, "No, and how do you know all this shit?"

Bruce glances over at Forbes before squarely looking at me and smugly offering, "Because I do my homework. You mean you accepted an invitation to integrate into a black school in Atlanta, Georgia without knowing why or what for."

"Shit man, I didn't even know it was a black school until after I got here," I am surprised at the defensive edge in my voice.

"Yeah, you couldn't tell anything from the award letter. But I knew it was a black school before I got here. I looked it up in a directory of universities. It's ranked pretty good so I said, 'What the hell' but I'm beginning to wonder," Bruce offers.

Forbes rolls his bloodshot eyes skyward, "Did you two pick up on the hostility in that little gathering? Well, that little gathering consists of your classmates. There were supposed to be ten fellowships. It looks like the others are gonna be late arrivals or else, no shows. For safety, if for no other reason we better keep close to each other. Where are you staying Duane?"

"In the dorm—Room 238."

"What?" Forbes blurts loudly incredulously looking at me. "You gotta be shitting us. I think coming on campus for classes is one thing, but you won't catch my ass this side of Peachtree after dark."

Bruce nods in agreement, "Of course, I'm married with two kids so any thought of staying on campus is out. I found a nice two-bedroom apartment in DeKalb County. How about you Forbes?"

"For social reasons more than safety I got a little studio up in the Buckhead area. I'm not letting anyone know the address until I scope things out better." He takes a long drag and inhales deeply, releasing smoke from his nose and mouth as he turns to me and adds, "But there are quite a few closer in by Georgia State, if you're interested," Forbes indicates.

"Nah—I'm moved in and besides I can't afford it. I'm not worried about a social life; I just want to get a master's degree and get the hell out of here."

"Man, you're crazy. These Georgia peaches are mighty fine and they like guys who are going to college. It's a big deal down here."

"I've got a girlfriend back in Montana. I'm not going to complicate my relationship with Loretta by chasing around down here."

"Hell man, I'm with Forbes. If I weren't married, I'd look forward to nonintellectual distractions with some of these fine chicks. Johnson, I can tell already that you take life too seriously. I just hope you don't wake up dead in your dorm room some morning—with your throat slit ear to ear. I force myself to avoid shuddering at this thought. Talking about getting serious for a moment, what classes are you guys planning to take?"

Forbes looks over to see if I am going to speak, and seeing my dead-pan look, hesitantly says, "I'm going to see if I can take some independent study courses. But one thing's for sure, I'm going to stay away from Cothran. He sounds like he still believes in human sacrifice."

"Not me," Bruce asserts. "It sounds like he runs the show and I think it's better to get to know him and what he wants rather than try to finesse him. Hey, let's say we go to the library and look over what they gave us in these packets."

Looking at his watch, Forbes says, "Sounds like a good idea but I gotta get across town and get some work done on my car."

"I'll go with you but I don't think the library is the place to talk. How about my room?"

Bruce says, "Hell no, I'm not going to invite trouble by hanging around a black dorm. Let's say whoever gets here first in the morning saves a place for the other two and we can see what we got then."

"That's okay with me," Forbes flips his cigarette onto the grass and pulls a set of keys from his pocket.

"See you guys," I say as both Bruce and Forbes head toward the parking lot together, adjourning the huddle.

Sept. 21, 1967

Hi Lorreta:

I just got up, too late for breakfast and too early to go to the library. I have 42 papers to do on different concepts of sociological theory so I am going to start right now and knock them out. Besides that, we must develop two of the papers into major thesis—pain, pain. That's for one class. I have term papers coming out my ears.

I have made arrangements to pick my mail up at a friend's house. He is another white person here doing his grad work. You can imagine how I felt when I saw him on campus. He is married with two kids and lives in a suburb. So at least I can escape from this ghetto once in a while and visit with some friends. His address is:

Oxford House Apts.
4903 Riverdale Rd., Apt. 19D
College Park, Georgia 30032

If you have time you can drop me a card—you better have time! I must get to the library now. Hope to have a better attitude and more time so I can write you a decent letter this weekend.

All is well. Take care of yourself and get out and have some fun.

Love ya,
Duane

September 22, 1967

Dear Folks,

I don't know if I told you but I ran into another white guy whose name is Bruce Stone. He is married and lives in a suburb. Because of the mass confusion here at the University I am going to have all my mail sent to his address. He seems to

be an honest person so please do not hesitate to send any mail
to me at this address:

Oxford House Apts.
4903 Riverdale Rd., Apt. 19D
College Park, Georgia 30032

You can pass this address along to Bob Kaste and anyone from
the college who might ask about me. It might be a good idea
to send to me in care of him in case there is any mix-up at the
apartments. It is a very large unit and is quite complex.

Please call Joyce Walker and give her my address. She might be
a little hesitant to write first so send me her address.

I have decided to remain on campus, at least this semester. I
am close to the library and have so much research work to do
that I don't want to get sidetracked on some social life I might
find off campus. Also, there is some question whether or not I
am eligible for the GI benefits since the government is putting
up the money for my fellowship. If I am not eligible, I won't be
able to afford to buy a car and support myself in an apartment.

Tell Bonny that I sure am glad I have the handkerchiefs she
gave me. I am continuously mopping my face. The heat is
almost unbearable, and they say it is quite cool here now—
bull crap!

I have a rather decent schedule. I have three evening classes
and one on Saturday. The rest are spread thru the week. In one
class I have 42 term papers and two major theses. Man, can
you imagine trying to work and getting that done. That is in

one class. I haven't received definite assignments in the rest yet but I know term papers will be expected in all. More bull crap!

I am in good health and in fair spirits. Time is going fast. I will soon be home for Christmas—that is if I get my work done.

Love to all,
Duane

6

Wake-Up Call

The Georgia sun has taken over the day. There is no longer that fresh morning damp smell with the invasion of smoke from extinguished fires. The warmth of the sun on my back feels good. It's as though someone greater is wrapping their arms around me, assuring me all is well. The sun quiets my thoughts as I walk in and out of the patches of shaded sidewalk. I don't dwell on the notion of being joined by other whites and their concerns. After all, I am here to get an education, and for no other reason.

I wonder if enough courses will be offered to support a major in Industrial Sociology or will I need to change my area of study. While it's not as high profile as Race Relations or the Sociology of Poverty, much research and commentary are needed to focus on the maturing industrial base here in the United States. Swedish, German, and even French sociologists are far ahead when it comes to knowing the effects of change, aging populations, and technology. I have pretty much decided to focus on research as a skill area. I must major in whatever will grant me a MA from this institution.

I once again notice the neatness of the houses and yards that line Chestnut Street. The houses look like they were built prior to World War II, since they are adorned with verandas, gables, and front porches, which disappeared in home construction amidst the building boom that was fed by returning veterans. The neighborhood reminds me of the lower, south side of Great Falls. Boulevards of shade trees and trimmed lawns that cover Mother Earth with a blanket of green, I somehow feel very much at home here on Chestnut Street. There is an ever so subtle invasion of my nostrils by a faint but familiar smell. My mind wanders looking for a memory bank that will reveal what the smell represents. My eyes search for clues for what the sweet spicy aroma might be. Then I spot the open doorway, guarded only by a green-painted screen door. Yes, definitely, it's the pleasant smell of pies baking that steals its way out of the kitchen, through the living room, and into the street. I guess it could be apple pie or pumpkin—something sweet with a hint of cinnamon. For an instant my nostrils take charge and I feel like bouncing onto the porch, whereupon a huge piece of piping hot pie would be served up. I smile as my stomach reminds me it's close to lunchtime.

Halfway out of my fantasy, my peripheral vision catches a girl with light-colored-skin and shiny black hair approaching. Clutching a binder to her breast, she's wearing a warm smile across her finely sculpted face. She must also be in range of the seductive kitchen fragrance. Then suddenly her eyes shift upward and her gaze meets mine. As if she's been slapped in the face, her expression changes. Her eyes narrow, her mouth turns down, and with her face glares with repulsive hate. She doesn't look away as we pass one another. I can't imagine what's taken a hold of her as her dark eyes fixate on me—it is the first hate stare that has pierced my protective veneer of naivety. Her look wasn't one of disapproval like you might feel when committing some social faux pas. This gaze was more penetrating.

I reach Ware Hall, and once in my room, I shut and lock the door. My hands are shaking uncontrollably. Perspiration soaks my shirt—mostly under my arms but across my chest areas as well. I've never felt this way before. In spite of the profuse sweating, my forehead feels cold and I'm experiencing a light-headed, floating sensation. My stomach growls but

I have no desire to eat. Not only do I doubt I'd be able to choke anything down, but I'm in no mood to sit and be stared at—and how many of those stares will be the same hate stare which I'm still staggering from. I decide to skip lunch.

I must be losing it. I never remember going through the number of emotional swings as this morning's has brought. Neither can I remember such highs and lows. Wow! I better get a hold of myself or I'll never see a master's degree. I must stop examining her intention—real or imagined. I need to remain focused on the reason I'm here—education—okay.

I go through the packet of material received this morning. There's an Atlanta University catalog; a separate sheet of department requirements to be eligible for a master's candidacy, and five class sign-up cards. Two full semesters of a Sociology Seminar are required, so I fill out one of the five cards, accordingly. Three other required courses are only scheduled in the fall—so I register for Elementary Statistics with Conyers, Methods of Research with Williams, and the Study of Society. Cothran is listed as the professor for the latter, a survey course on theoretical fundamentals. This leaves one class card to be filled out. I look for anything in industrial sociology. There is only one course called Complex Organizations that comes close. T.C. Cothran is the noted professor so I decide not to give him sole power to expunge me from the program and instead sign up for The Family taught by C. McDaniels, PhD. Oh well, so much for a major in Industrial Sociology. It looks like Sociology will have to be my major. "Ever adaptable" will have to be my middle name. Recalling Forbes's sworn strategy to stay clear of Cothran makes me smile. I pick up my towel and head for the showers, hoping to cool my body, which is feeling and smelling the worse for wear.

When I return to my room, I feel clean but fatigued. A little nap will complement the shower to achieve the sense of refreshment that I had this morning.

When I wake up, the sun is below the tree lines and long shadows are cast across the track field outside my window. It's 8:15 p.m.—crap! I've missed supper! Fearing a migraine if I go too long on an empty stomach, I head for the dayroom's candy machines.

The seven students, all male, could be seventeen for the noise and carrying on which fills the dayroom as I enter. Four boisterous players are hard at what must be a high-stakes call shot game if the kibitzing and coaching are any indication. Two are watching TV and another is standing, watching the game at one moment, and the TV the next. I can't hear the TV when I first enter. But by the time I'm in front of the Coke machine, one voice drops off followed by another until the only voice I hear is Matt Dillon's in *Gunsmoke*. Cokes are ten cents here. They only cost five cents back home. The candy selection is meager, probably because the heat will turn most chocolate bars into a soupy mess. Damn, ten cents for a Payday. That also only costs five cents back home.

I sit, sipping my Coke and devouring my caramel, honey, and pea-nut-studded candy bar and watch the pool game—which is now a quiet, somber affair. I guess the game is slop rotation after watching a few shots.

It's not their quiet treatment but the stifling stale air in the dayroom that makes me decide to finish my Coke outside. The screen door does little to quiet the fracas that escapes through its mesh.

The oncoming darkness makes it difficult to distinguish the debaters from onlookers in the assembly of the dozen or so in the dayroom. Half are in shorts with no shirts. Now and again an onlooker will utter a 'right on.'

Some are agreeing with all that is said so it is hard to determine which side has the most support.

"Let the motherfuckers go to one of their own schools. What makes them think they will be welcome here after the way we've been treated?"

"Sounds like you're wanting to keep things segregated."

"You motherfucking right I do—at least our schools and our churches. Wherever you let the devil in he'll take over."

"Well sounds like you must be from Alabama—the governor there got coloreds and whites thinking segregation forever—that's where we've been man—that's not what we want for the future."

"Who says? We ain't gonna get nothing but shit jobs and shit pay from the devil. If Civil Rights are going to work, we got to have equal treatment, equal jobs. And those jobs are going to come from our own institutions and businesses."

"Fuck integration. You integrate whites and they will take it all and leave you the crumbs."

"Man—next you're gonna have all us get aboard a ship to go to Africa."

"Fuck no—that's not what I'm saying. We helped build this fuckin country—why should we leave. I'm for Black Power here in this country."

"Then how you gonna keep whites away?"

"We can take the Southern half and let the whites keep the Northern half. They like it cold anyway."

"Now bro—you really got yourself a plan. How are you gonna talk anyone into giving half the country to ten percent of the population. You're fuckin stupid, man."

"Well, maybe we could settle on Texas and California."

"A new country—no way man, I want Georgia and Florida, you can keep Texas."

"Why you want to live on this heap of farmed-out clay. It's not good for nothing anymore. At least Texas has oil."

"Well, let's not fight over something that ain't gonna happen in a million years. I say King and Farmer are right—we need to get our piece of the pie from the same trough whitey gets his."

"I don't think Farmer and King agree on that."

"Who cares? They both nothing but house niggers for White Power, anyway."

"Man, you talking shit."

"No matter—my argument is with the sons of the devil who gonna take space and attention. Why in the hell are they coming here?"

"Why don't you ask one of them, he's coming back in right now."

To me— "Why did you pick Atlanta University?" Oscar inquires.

"The federal government picked the school."

"Then, why are you here?" Oscar continues to probe.

"Cause the government is paying for my books, tuition, and fees."

Cy laughs, "Ha, ha—now who's gonna turn down *the Man*'s money? The government paying you to spy?" Cy asks.

"No."

Cy continues, "Are you gonna try and take over?"

"No."

"I bet you gonna haul ass as soon as you get your degree," comments Hector.

"Probably."

Hector continues, "Where to—where's home?"

"Montana."

"Why don't you go to Montana State?" questions Cy.

"I can't afford it."

"Hey, hey—guess the dudes are doing it to you, too," Cy laments.

"Don't take this personally," I state trying to assure the crowd.

"Bullshit—I want every devil—well-intended or not to take this personally. Every blood brother is affected personally."

"Motherfucker, where you get off—don't take this personally."

I finished my Coke ten minutes ago. I sit quietly hoping the subject will shift—at least I hope attention is diverted from me for long enough so I can leave the dayroom without giving the impression of retreating.

The theme and arguments are repeated redundancies. Some are having fun. Some are angrily involved. I am taken aback by how vociferous and pointed the verbal attacks can be without physical violence erupting. I wonder what it would take to ignite mob actions. Some booze, another degree or two warmer, someone talking out of turn—not much—I guess.

I stand, then turn and walk slowly toward my room when three students returning from Hunter Street walk through the agitated circle in the dayroom. I listen for any expression of protest as I withdraw. None are noted. First to fade are the dissidents, then even the loudest of the pontificators becomes just noise.

The quiet of my room mitigates the late summer heat. The only window is open as far as it will go. I decide against leaving my door open to catch whatever draft might stir the stifling air. I try reading but hardly get through any of Georg Simmel's *The Dyad and Triad* before the green walls seem to absorb the light and my eyes become scratchy and watery.

I can hear some men in the track area doing what sounds like a close order drill. The commands and cadence seem out of place. I surmise that it must be a ROTC group connected with Morehouse or Spelman. The quiet marching seems to go on forever when suddenly the practicing shifts as the squad or platoon all start to growl and grunt together. I can't imagine what drill could be punctuated in this manner. Maybe it's some form of jujitsu, or bayonet thrusts, or some type of commando exercise. My mind wanders from the pages and away from the chorus of commando grunts to something I'd read about colored soldiers being night fighters. I wonder if Negroes can see better at night than white soldiers. My curiosity is peaked enough to make a mental note to ask Lonnie.

I finally give up any pretense of reading and return the theory book to its place on the shelf above my desk. I turn on my radio alarm and search for a station with music or a message that will soothe the homesickness creeping over me. I am amazed by how many AM stations I can pick up. One has a myriad of choices compared to the four stations in Great Falls. I finally get a clear signal and listen to a Country Western song like the music played on KMON Great Falls. The disc jockey is playing a mix of requests as well as his own selections. The twangy lyrics of *Thunder Road* remind me again of where I am and how faraway the mountains of Montana are. I lay naked on my bed. Habit has me pull the sheet over me but I soon find even its thin layer is too warm. I kick off the sheet and lay on my back waiting for the sandman to provide some respite from the heat.

There is a seemingly constant cry of sirens. I wonder about the goings-on in a city like Atlanta that could cause so many crises. I begin to discern the differences between the sirens near and far. I guess the long, whining sirens are ambulances carrying the carnage of misspent humans. I then hear two or three different quick-pulsing sirens that I guess are law enforcement from one jurisdiction or another. Some of these are short-lived; others wail until drowned out by the distance. Fire engines blare a mix of long wails punctuated by several rapid-fire cries interrupted now and again with a blast of what sounds like foghorns. I imagine all of Atlanta ablaze from the number of noisy runs made by the city's fire brigades. I nervously sniff the air to test for the approach of Armageddon.

Repeated playing's of *Thunder Road* join the constant chorus of sirens maybe four times before the station signs off by playing the National Anthem. I look at the radio clock, it registers 12:30 a.m. And the sirens wail on preventing sleep from entering my tired being. The events, mood, and length of the day have taken their toll on both my mind and body. My sleepless mind replays the tapes of the day and leaves me wondering what price will be extracted for this 'free' education.

The black inkiness outside my window begins to fade ever so softly before birds of an unknown species begin to join the city's night song. The birds have a calming effect as the sirens fade.

I am only half-awake when there's a knock at my door. "Who is it?"

"Lonnie."

"Just a minute," I roll out of bed and put on shorts and jeans before opening the door.

Lonnie's wearing a pair of striped blue and red pajamas. Mostly blue with red pinstripes but loud enough to make me wonder how anyone can sleep in such a getup.

"What's happening, Lonnie?"

"I wonder if you'd mind going over the course schedule with me? This catalog has me snookered." Lonnie's holding the catalog with the course sign-up cards marking the place where the School of Sociology lists its offerings.

"Yeah, okay, but not until I get something to eat and some coffee. I missed supper last night and my stomach thinks my throat has been cut."

"Do they have any orange juice down there?" Lonnie asks.

Guessing, I say, "Yeah."

"Let me get dressed and I'll join you."

Sunday September 24, 1967

Dear Folks,

Well things have settled down and I kinda know what is expected of me here. It is a lot and I don't know exactly how I'm going to get the job done but I'll have to give it my best. All of my professors are PhDs and talk a language all of their own. They say the flunk out rate here is tremendous the first semester so I might be coming home around the first of the year.

It is a little too noisy to study right now so thought it is a good time to send home a few words. I studied the other night until about 6:30 p.m., then I was going to rest a while -- I woke up at 6:30 the next morning. Guess I had been going on my nerves. I didn't realize I was so pooped. I feel really good. The weather has been unbelievable –real warm. I don't wear a T-shirt because it is too warm. The food here in the dorm is great. They have a choice of meats, salads and desserts every meal. I have decided to stay in the dorm at least for this semester, because it is close to the library and I'm a little afraid I would be tempted to start neglecting my studies.

I heard Martin Luther King address a crowd last Sunday here in Atlanta. They are having a problem of double-shifting the

Negro children in schools and are appealing for a more equal system. His speech was delivered at the West Hunter Street Baptist Church which is about three blocks from the dorm. I understand he gives about 450 speeches a year and of course his most famous public speech is "I Have a Dream" delivered in 1963. I am happy I was able to take advantage of this while in Atlanta. This weekend the Muslims had a rally in the neighborhood but I didn't go. No honkeys (Whites) are allowed. It is quite an experience to be here and get in on the action at the grass roots level instead of listening to the television news reports.

I am enclosing a check for $22. Please put it in the savings account. I would like to know how much I have in the account right now so I can budget myself accordingly. I will probably want a new car when I get home so will try and be real conservative. Did you ever contact Bob Kaste and pay him the $50 that I owe his sister for the clothes I bought in Big Sandy? If not, please do, and say hello to his ma and sister and all for me. —Thanks!

Give my love to all. I miss Montana very much.
Duane

9/26/67

Dear Sweet Pea,

Loretta, Loretta, Loretta…please forgive me for misspelling your name all this time. No excuse, I'm just a retard is all.

77

I was really in another world when I received your first letter. You don't know how low my morale was at the time. There is lots of work ahead of me but I think maybe I can endure.

I appreciate what you said about having difficulty saying something meaningful on paper. When I write you, I'm embarrassed to mail what I have managed to blast out. It seems superficial and inadequate. I hope that you can read between the lines because there my true feelings are hidden. Oh boy, am I getting mystical. Good-looking, I love you in a very special way and I pray that I will be fortunate to be the one to make you a very happy woman, some day. I miss being able to talk to you and being able to hold you close. You always made me feel powerful when I could squeeze you. Well, maybe someday again!!!

Kid, (oh, oh, you don't like that) I have a night class to make so will have to rush off. I'll write a more informative letter this weekend. Bye for now...

All my love,
Duane

7

The Grind Begins

After dressing, I knock on Lonnie's door. He seems anxious and invites me into his room. He motions for me to sit down. He says, "I have been thinking that you are playing dumb but I am coming to the realization that your lack of knowledge of my people stems from Montana being out of touch due to distance." He seems eager to unlock my ignorance. I'm embarrassed but forced to see my opportunity is to be an attentive listener.

I stutter, "Lonnie, are you sharing knowledge that took place during the time of slavery or post-slavery."

"The shit I am sharing with you began the moment the slaves stepped off the ship and continues until this moment. Believe it or not nothing has changed that much. One of the persistent sins against the slaves was starvation. The plantation owners didn't care about nutrition and the health of the slaves as long as they could do their work. Another persistent discrimination against are the police and their treatment toward the Negro. This is one of the sins that continues to this day—there's a long-standing anger about police brutality. With the end of slavery, many of the Negroes were shoved off the plantations and had to find a way to feed themselves outside of the plantation. In the South, the end of slavery was replaced with 'separate but equal' which spelled out hopelessness with unemployment, poverty, bad schools, low home ownership rates, and the poorest of social services. Any violations of the 'separate but equal' standard was again dealt with by the white man's policemen. Travel for the Negro was very difficult in 'whites only' and 'colored' worlds of the freed Negroes." Lonnie's lesson in racial prejudice and sins continues.

"The whole of the Ku Klux Klan" he explains, "involved mostly illegal acts against the colored people. I know this shatters the protective shield for the white man's police force." Lonnie finally takes a breath and states, "This is enough for today."

"Wow, Lonnie I am unaware of so much of your past."

Lonnie states, "Let's go."

We head down for breakfast as I am still grasping to understand his anger. After breakfast, Lonnie says he'll catch up with me at our first class— Dr. Conyers's statistics class. As I approach Dr. Conyers's classroom, I hear the unruly gossip of the students long before the doorway to the classroom. The gossip and banter cease almost immediately as I enter the room. I take a seat near the back of the room and can feel the embarrassed silence as a result of my presence. After a couple minutes, Dr. Conyers storms into the room and heads for the lecture podium; he looks over the class and says, "Now that's the kind of respectful quiet a professor enjoys."

Most of the class turns and looks my way. Conyers follows their eyes, which land on me sitting near the back of the room, and says, "Oh, now I understand."

The statistics class is made up of about twenty-five students. He lists the title of the required text and the chapters and problems to solve by the next class. Conyers says, "If there are no questions, we will meet next Monday, same time and classroom. Everyone understands that this is graduate-level statistics. I don't believe in taking attendance; I've learned that for me to get to know you it's best if you announce your name when answering or asking questions. That's about it."

As I quickly get up to leave, I wonder if the next class will be this brief. My next class is Sociology of the Family taught by Dr. Clyde McDaniels. McDaniels is already standing behind a paper-covered podium that reaches nearly to the height as McDaniels himself. He waits the full ten minutes for students to settle in their seats. McDaniels welcomes us to what he calls, "One of the most important classes for gaining an insight into the plight of the Southern Negro." He asserts, "There is a clear distinction between white American families and black urbanized families. First, the black family is normally headed by a mother, grandmother, aunt, or some other female provider. Seldom will you find a black male that is consistently a part of the black family. He's usually walking the streets to hustle for money to support the family. Most of the matriarchs have accomplished more schooling than their black brothers. School is considered a waste of time in the myriad of things that need to be accomplished on the street. It makes for an easy and understandable exit from schoolwork. From time to time, the brothers' absence is due to confinement in state or federal penitentiaries. Many, if not most moneymaking opportunities are outlawed and closely policed by the white man's protector."

McDaniel's lecture goes the full fifty minutes without any interrupting questions or comments. As the bell rings, McDaniels raises his hands in a posture to get our attention about something important, "There will be a midterm and a final exam plus a paper delving into the differences between these two-family structures due at the end of the semester." (There's a collective groan from the class and many will claim they never heard about the term paper's due date.)

My theory course is scheduled for 7:30 p.m., so I return to my dorm room to catch up on some reading. I end up falling asleep and damn if I don't sleep until after the start of class. Of course, it is pouring rain, grabbing my hooded rain jacket, textbook, and notebook and head as quickly as possible to Dr. Cothran's class. My entrance interrupts a conversation between Cothran and several students resulting in silence that continues as I sheepishly locate an empty seat. As I sit down and remove my jacket, the class begins to snicker. Cothran asks, "What brings you to class at this hour?"

I explain, "I fell asleep after dinner and here I am—as I know the first class should not be missed."

It turns out that the conversation I interrupted was a debate whether Negroes' posture, walk, and stature is learned or innate. One of the student debaters says, "That's Duane. He's been hanging with Lonnie so much that he is starting to shuffle and walk like him. I think it's a set-up deal."

Cothran says, "No, not by your professor. What we have just learned by this debate is that theories can often be questionable. With that and given the weather conditions outside, I am going to dismiss class early. Don't forget the forty-five term papers that were assigned at the beginning of class. Each concept chosen must be approached by three well-known sociologists."

There are many groans and expletives and more than one student asks, "Did I hear the professor correctly? Did he say forty-five term papers are due by the end of the course?"

October 4, 1967

Dear Folks,

I have just witnessed a racial brawl here in the dorm that made my blood run cold. It all started when one Negro called another a 'Nigger.' Of course, before it was over the heat of everyone's anger was turned on the Whites. Thank God that I had several friends that got me the hell out of there. These outbursts are frequent but usually just verbal. I do not involve myself at all, but I can't help being affected by the atmosphere. It bestows a climate that is not conducive to study—to say the least. I just hope I can conquer this feeling of animosity that has its grips on me.

I received your letter and it sure was great to hear from all of you. Be sure, to tell Kent and Kim hello from their uncle. And I was really tickled to hear that Dad had been on the bike. He can sure feel welcome to get all the use out of it that he can. Oh yes, I wrote Terry a letter and gave them my address. I sure hope they have time to write. It is the only motivation I have—knowing that I have people somewhere that are interested in my success. Personally, I could care less.

Please be careful when you pay those gas bills. Make sure there are slips of proof that I made the purchase. Sometimes they add someone else's balance onto mine, but I just pay what I actually owe them and they straighten it out by next month or so. That one sounded kinda high. But no matter—thanks a million for taking care of all my problems back there. I am enclosing a check for $245. Forty-five is to be put in the bank. I still had money left from the $500 that I took with me so will bank this. If I run short, I will call for a money order. Please advise me of my financial status again when you write.

It is hard for me to realize that Dad will be hunting in a couple weeks. The weather is still unforsakenly hot down here. I don't think the temperature is more than about 85 degrees but the humidity makes you think you have just walked into a steam bath. But all the same, I have a slight case of hunting fever. Damn—wonder when I am going to stop all this messing

*around and have one good year of nothing but hunting
and fishing.*

*Well Folks, guess I will hit the sack. Kinda too tense to study
tonight. Please say hello to all from me and tell them I'm
making it. Please apologize to Terry and Bonny—I really don't
have a minute to spare and I hope they can include themselves
as part of 'my folks back home' so these letters can be regarded
as written to them. I suppose since Bonny is working, she won't
be needing money for shoes so I guess I won't be hearing from
her. Now, I'm just kidding Goudie.*

Love you all,
Duane

October 8, 1967

Hi Loretta,

*I'm taking a break so thought I would drop you a line. I have
two tests Monday; one in Statistics and one in Methods and
Research. Both are my weakest courses. After hearing from you,
I went and finished a term paper that had me down. I still have
44 to go but the first one is always the tough one. I don't think
it's an 'A' but it's done and that's good enough for me.*

*Yesterday, I was coming out of the library and saw two Negro
kids run up and grab this girl's purse. I took out after them but
they left me in their dust. I returned to see if the girl was okay
and asked her how much was in the purse. She had just gotten
a payment from her fellowship and had over $200 in the purse.
She called the police and was told she was the second victim*

84

that day on the campus. Nice place! I told you they have armed guards after dark. Twice, I have heard gunshots. You had better believe I don't leave the dorm after the sun goes down.

I have found a radio station that plays country music and I listen to it all the time. It reminds me of Montana and when I think of Montana (God's country) I always think of you.

Started getting mushy so I'll change the subject. Say Sweet Pea, did you ever get to see an eye doctor? You know you should see one once a year, especially wearing contacts and ones that irritate you! I know you will be too proud to wear glasses on campus but you could wear them while you studied in your room. Oh well, you're a big girl and know what's best.

So, you think I should wait for the new Corvette Stingray? I won't get it until June or there about. And I don't think I have much of a break between semesters. I just looked it up. I get ten days from the 1st of June until the tenth. That would give me time to fly home and pick up the car and maybe even get to see you. Well, I'm not worrying about things that far away. I'm more concerned about how this semester will come out and if we will be able to see lots of each other this Christmas.

Well Good-looking, must rush. Take good care of yourself and be happy. You are a very fortunate young lady. You are intelligent and very good-looking. And it hasn't spoiled your personality. Very few people have so many important attributes. And don't be concerned about me—I still do and always will regardless. If I'm not the most desirable person in the world to communicate with, don't think it's because I don't care. I care very much—very, very much. But it seems

a little phony to sit and tell a piece of paper that I love you.
Enough said!

The nameless one in Georgia,
Dew

Sunday, October 15, 1967

Greetings Sweet Pea,

Gee, I was so shocked to hear your problems concerning the
mishap with the fellow on the motorcycle that I don't think I
was very reassuring. I was glad that Jane was there with you.
Experiences like that are especially hard to face alone. By now I
hope its old news.

The weather down here is still very warm and humid. It's really
hard to believe. I still wear short sleeve shirts to class – nothing
else. It's probably a good thing that I don't have my Sting-ray
here. I get strong urges to just get behind a wheel of a car and
go. And I mean go!

I am a little behind the schedule that I put myself on for writing
term papers. So, I will be staying up tonight and pounding
away. I want to have all term papers finished before Christmas
so I can really relax and not have anything to worry about.
I have had a couple of quizzes and have done pretty good
in everything except Statistics. I have had no background in
Statistics and I'm kinda lost. Hope to be able to straighten
myself out though. School work is not what you call really
tough but there is so much of it. I will have to start going to the
library at night if I'm going to get the work done.

Most of the guys that are in school are really nice. There are only a few Black Nationalists who preach hate and revolution and I stay away from them. And I stay away from the ghetto people as much as possible. I got a hair cut in a ghetto barber shop and was surprised about the way I was treated. They just don't want whitey down here. – And this is one whitey that is gonna oblige them first chance I get.

Well, Good-looking, how is Bozeman? I hope you are all caught up with the classes you missed and can relax a bit. I sure hope you have a good time in school – it's your last semester and you'll never have another chance like this. Naturally, I hope you know what I mean by fun. You don't have to do anything degrading or immoral to have fun ... I think. Course I'm old fashioned. Anyway, I know that you have excellent judgement and will never do anything foolish. – Now, what the hell am I getting so moralistic for all of a sudden. Forget it ... OK? I'm beginning to worry about myself a little. I think I'm getting senile. Oops! Out of paper. Bye for now – take care of yourself.

Love ya,
Dew

xoxoxo

8

Day Of Rest And Unrest

Lonnie and I miss the Sunday meal, which leads to a discussion of whether it would be appropriate for us to eat on Hunter Street. We agree that we should be fine together. Lonnie tells me to be on my toes since we are walking down the main drag of pickpockets, brown baggers, and other hustlers on this 'famous' street. As we pass a pool hall, one of the several guys standing around the open doors asks me if I have any matches. I go through my pockets, trying to accommodate his request. After a thorough search, I apologize saying that I guess I left my matches in the room. Lonnie and I continue and maybe get a half-a-dozen steps past the clicking balls on the green felt billiard tables when Lonnie stops abruptly and turns toward the man that asked for matches, and says "Hey, you aren't as smooth as you think you are. Give his wallet back *now*." Lonnie's voice has the sting of a command.

The match moocher agrees saying, "We were just playing a little game," and offers my wallet he had just lifted from my shirt pocket.

Lonnie says, "Stealing a man's money is no game where I come from. You're lucky you don't get shot being as amateur as you are." Lonnie grabs the wallet and looks through it, counting the $20.00 and says to me, "Looks like you are buying dinner. Is that all you had?"

"Yes," I quickly respond.

As we continue down Hunter Street, other blacks chastise Lonnie for hanging with a honky. Lonnie asserts independence, rationalizing, "He's no honky, he's from Montana."

Later, once Lonnie and I finished dinner, we start walking back to Ware Hall, when we see a gathering of four or five males ahead standing on the right side of the street. Lonnie anxiously yells at me, "You need to head back without me and make sure you walk on the left side of the street." I don't understand but hurry back away from the crowd.

Once back in my room, I start working on one of the lengthy term papers, and become so involved that I forgot what had transpired earlier with Lonnie. I decide to take a break and head out. I walk toward some of the residents who are gathered down the hallway. Cy quickly yells, "Lonnie was just shot in the groin by a guy in a passing car."

Shocked by the news, I ask, panicking, "Is he going to be okay? Did they catch the shooter? Do you know why Lonnie got shot?"

Hector, who goes by Hector the Greek, tries to explain, "They don't have a lead on the guy who did the shooting but there's all sorts of speculation about why he was shot. Some think it was mistaken identity or that it was someone from Cleveland looking for revenge to settle some score. Lonnie carried a gun but the shot happened so quickly that he didn't have a chance to get off a shot. Some people said that the brothers on the sidewalk were there to distract him."

"Hector, do you think Lonnie got shot because he's been hanging out with me?"

"No, the people that hate you and all other honkies would have shot you and not Lonnie!"

I nod, as Hector continues. "You probably don't know why Lonnie is here. He had the chance to accept a fellowship to attend graduate school or go to prison. He knew that he had a mark on his head—he left some pretty unhappy people back in Cleveland."

"Is … is he going to be out of the hospital soon?" I stammer.

"Last word I got is that it was a bad shot and he probably won't make it back to school this semester but he'll get to finish school. He's going to be all right, Dew."

Shaken, I feel really anxious and want to talk to Loretta. Fortunately, I have the right amount of change for the public phone jiggling in my pocket and I approach the phone booth. Immediately, after hearing her calm voice and taking a few breaths, my mind quits rushing. My propensity for short telephone conversations is always at odds with Loretta's desire to continue to profess our love in lengthy and expensive phone calls. So, after a brief explanation, I start to hang up when I'm startled by a quick rapping on the glass door. Thinking that this brother is anxious to get me off the phone so he can talk to his girlfriend, I nod indicating that I'm getting off, when he suddenly pulls out a pistol! I yell into the phone, "Loretta, I need to get off the phone now! There's a guy with a gun either looking for me or who needs to use the phone immediately."

Once I hang up and hurriedly leave the booth, the intruder identifies himself as campus security. "Sorry sir," I quickly say.

"No, no man it is just that I gotta call the cops to help us capture this bad ass," he explains.

Meanwhile, I return to my room, uttering to myself that I have to remember to call and explain this to Loretta. Days pass before we talk again.

The following weekend I call Loretta and she begins to cry upon hearing my voice. "What's wrong, sweetheart?"

"I thought you were dead," She cries out. "Please Duane quit and come home."

Wednesday, October 25, 1967

Dear Magnolia Blossom,

I just got back from taking a test. I didn't even know I was going to have one until I walked into class. I skip this methods class because all the professor ever talks about is his dissertation, and I have term papers coming out of my ears. I have done twelve and have 33 left to go. I don't know if I'll be able to hack it. But the test this morning didn't hurt me. He came right from the book and I stay right up to date with my reading.

Lonnie Burton, the fellow that kinda showed me the ropes when I first got here is not doing too good. He was shot in the groin by a guy in a passing car. They do not have a lead on the guy who did the shooting but there are all sorts of speculation about why he got shot. Some think it was because he got too friendly with a honkie and others think it was a mistaken identity. I guess he was sort of a rebel rouser back in Cleveland and some think things there have caught up with him. I knew he carried a gun but thought it was because of racial tension... guess maybe it was.

They had a little excitement here the night before last. Some of my friends threw a Molotov Cocktail party. I am sending the clippings from one newspaper. The other paper had pictures but I can't find a copy of that one. I woke up about 1:30 AM to the sirens of the fire trucks and then heard all this noise – people hollering, glass breaking, etc. It was quite a show. But it is raining today – started yesterday so that will break up the 'party' atmosphere.

If you are wondering why the red print, I am afraid my ribbon has just about had it and I plan to type a term paper tonight so I want to save the black half – okay?

When I said goodbye to you on that beautiful September night in Montana, I wasn't sure if our relationship would last. The letters and few phone calls have changed my dreams regarding our future. I realize the importance of your faith and recognize my short but previous marriage lies between us. I haven't written up my case yet and know that it will take time and effort to be annulled. Kid, I was in such a mess when it came time to move down here that I didn't get to it. And now I'm in a bigger mess. I hope to be able to have it drafted at Christmas— as yet I haven't even contacted the old battle-axe (the ex). I will though—you realize she has to testify. In fact, much depends upon her testimony. Loretta, it is not easy to have to go back over all that mess again. I have almost succeeded in pushing it into oblivion. Well, I guess I will have to get some guts and face it.

This mess that I was part of is one reason I feel guilty even associating with you. That is why I would not feel bad if tomorrow you sent me your engagement announcement. Although I would feel suddenly very alone and empty, I would be happy for you. Somehow that is the only thing that really counts for you to be happy.

Hey – I gotta go to lunch. Some guys are waiting for me

BE HAPPY! I LOVE YOU!
The Dud

NEWSPAPER ARTICLE/THE ATLANTA JOURNAL

OCTOBER 23, 1967

REINFORCED POLICE CALM VINE CITY

By Alex Coffin

Helmeted policemen carrying shotguns and billy clubs moved into Vine City Monday night and dispersed more than 100 Negroes gathered on a playlot at Magnolia and Maple NW in the second night of racial unrest in that area.

Earlier, several young Negroes had broken into two stores and started small bon fires along Magnolia. They also broke out the rear window of a police car.

State Sen. Leroy Johnson, who with Ald. Q.V. Williamson and the Rev. Clyde Williams had moved through the crowd urging its members to return to their homes, was critical of the police action of moving in some 50 reinforcements.

Johnson had climbed atop a car and had just begun to speak to the Negroes when the police cars and wagons rolled in.

"Hold it! Hold it!" Johnson said to Capt. R. E. Little, who was leading the way.

"Hold it nothing. They're going to move right now," Little said.

As the Negroes protested, the policemen moved them on with their guns at port. Most of the Negroes ran down Magnolia shouting.

"Leave, damn it. Take 'em out. They're not going to listen to that," a Negro, who said his name was Roy Rose, shouted at the policemen.

"Sure, sure. You got 'em under control. Now move off the street," ordered Patrolman A.E. McKinnon.

"This is the worst thing that could have happened." Johnson said. "We had them under control."

Little said later that we would not have moved the reinforcements into the slum area had he known Johnson had most of the Negroes gathered on the playlot. "But a few minutes before when the window was knocked out, we determined the situation was out of control," he said. The rear window of Little's patrol car was smashed by a rock, which also struck Superintendent James F. Brown, head of the uniform division and coordinator of the police reinforcements, on the hand.

A meeting had been called for the playlot at 8 p.m., but it never materialized. Instead, Negroes, most of them teenagers and young adults, moved up and down Magnolia.

Many persons stood in their yards or on porches and watched.

A fire was started at the front doors of two grocery stores opposite each other at the Intersection of Magnolia and Vine streets, then later windows of the Big Rock Food Store at Walnut and Magnolia were smashed by flying rocks and bottles. Only a chain kept the surging crowd from entering the store. At about the same time, Negro youths broke down the door of Herman's Market at Magnolia and Maple.

After all the Negroes had returned to their homes and the area was quiet, fire broke out again, at one of the grocery stores and fire engines sped to the scene. Firemen said the second blaze was caused by a spark that hadn't been extinguished earlier.

A Negro woman, Mrs. Susie Mae Everett, was hit with a brick and broken glass when the brick crashed through the window of her second-story apartment above Herman's Market at 544 Magnolia St. NW. Police took her to Grady Hospital.

Meanwhile, several small fires were started in the streets and garbage cans. Newspaper vending boxes were pushed into the street.

Police cars continued to patrol the area, flashing spotlights, but rarely stopping.

Johnson and Williamson moved through the crowds urging them to go home. "What can this accomplish?" Johnson asked. "Let's go down to the Police Committee and do something about police brutality."

9

Surviving On And Off Campus

My attempt to live in Ware Hall has reached a breaking point! Enduring reverse discrimination, in the form of isolation, hate stares, silent treatment, and living as a white man in a "Black is Beautiful" world, provide real-life examples for my current area of study—sociology. What I can no longer endure are the 'ghost visitations.' They arrive during my study time and into the wee hours nearly every night. Although my room was ransacked on one occasion, I deduce fellow residents are trying to break up my study and sleep patterns, in an effort to lower my scores on quizzes and tests. My schedule is to study and write papers during the day and early evening and retire before 11:00 p.m. After dinner, I either lie on my bed and read or sit at the typewriter while attempting to finish a term paper when there's a knock on my door. I jump up and open the door to an empty hallway. After numerous attempts to catch the invisible intruder, I decide to sleep with earplugs during the daylight and early evening hours and work on term papers into the night, ignoring the many 'knock-knocks.' The 'ghost visitations' leave me alone on Saturday and Sunday probably because they have better plans.

On Sunday, without interruptions, I finally complete another paper, although I realize its past dining hours for Sunday brunch. I'm struck with a sudden hunger as my stomach growls. I decide to hit Hunter Street for take-out or a low-priced 'sit down' restaurant. Hunter Street is windy and pedestrians are few. I spot a take-out on the south side of Hunter. Seeing no queue outside, I stick my head in and see two people waiting for their orders to be filled. And in a flash, they are. Then, someone steps in front of me and orders a Number Three. After he has paid, I step up and ask, "My turn?"

The server shakes his head "no" and points his somewhat large carving knife at a sign posted next to an eight-foot by ten-foot menu. It reads, "We serve dark meat only!"

Not getting it, I cheerfully say, "That's okay with me, I would like an order of three legs."

The server looks at me with an incredulous hate stare—"Not here, honky!"

"Why?" I say a bit taken aback.

"Because the sign and I say so—get your sorry 'white devil' ass out of my shop!"

Without eating, I immediately leave for Ware Hall not looking back.

Later that evening feeling famished, I take a break from researching yet another term paper and go down to the dayroom for a chocolate bar. I find the usual two guys shooting pool and watching TV. A Sunday news channel has Governor Maddox ranting and raving about the ruination of the South because of the Yankee immigration. He describes the North migration, saying these Yankees have long hair and are touting hippie values. One of the pool players interrupts the diatribe and points to me, saying, "He's talking about you."

I respond defensively, "I may need a haircut but I am no way close to being a hippie."

The next morning, after eating breakfast, I shower and shave and come to the conclusion that I do need a haircut. I walk down Chestnut

Street and as I cross Hunter Street, I spot a barber shop next to the large landmark church. I walk in and find the barber cutting the hair of a brother, while a second brother sits reading a newspaper. Once the brother pays for his haircut and leaves the shop, the waiting brother jumps into the chair. Halfway through his haircut, another brother saunters in and takes an empty chair. When the barber's seat becomes vacant again, the latest arrival drops his magazine and places his bottom on the hair-cutting throne and says, "Not so close this time."

I think this guy must have a prearranged appointment since the barber didn't motion that I was next.

The barber responds, "I can do that." He doesn't acknowledge my presence. Soon I'm alone with the barber and he states emphatically, "I know how to cut straight hair. When I was in the army, I learned the white man's haircut. But if I cut a white man's hair, while I own this neighborhood shop, they will boycott me or worse burn me out." He continues, suggesting that I might get my hair cut if I went across the bridge.

That night, I decide to go get a drink at The Birdcage, a world-class nightclub, just a few blocks from Ware Hall. I seat myself at an empty table and nod to the cocktail waitress, indicating I want to order a drink. After a long wait and watching her serve several other cocktails, she informs me, "I've been told by the bartender, I can only serve you if you do not cause any disturbance."

I say, "Fine by me. I just want to order a glass of beer on tap."

She proclaims, "We serve bottles only."

I savor my beer and listen to the band playing a Blues/Jazz number that I don't recognize. Finishing my beer, I sit and listen to the soulful, pristine jazz. Noticing that the colored waitress has passed my table several times with drinks for other customers and there are few empty tables left, I move to the bar and ask the bartender, "Could I get another beer?"

He responds, "You might try the club down the street, their beer is cold and less pricey, absent music."

"I get the message," I respond heading back toward Ware Hall.

Saturday, Oct. 28, 1967

Dear Loretta;

Howdy 'kid!' How's things in God's country? Man, do I wish I could be up in cow country right now. This rebel territory is hurting.

I have been looking for a car and a place to stay, and would you believe it – everything, and I mean everything is higher down here. I have someone to move in with but I don't want to make the move until I get a car. I don't like to depend on anybody to be a taxi driver for me. And I found out that cars rust out very fast here so I don't want to buy a very good car and it's hard to find a clunker that is reliable. I will give it another try Tuesday. I blew the whole weekend – hmm, I keep forgetting that today is Saturday. This guy from Atlanta was helping me look around, and I offered to buy him a beer. So, we went into a working man's bar (if you know what I mean – nothing fancy) known as The Bucket of Blood, and had a glass. Fifty cents – for a stinking glass of beer! You know I'll lose my beer belley (sic) now! You would think I would know how to spell belly (?) after all the griping you do about mine. Well I still have it! At least you will be able to recognize me at Christmas.

Even if you won't speak. (I'm referring to the letter you sent
– chewing me out for not writing.) Really Sweet Pea, I'M
REALLY TIED DOWN TO STUDIES! I am trying to get to
work on my theses. When I finish my course studies in August,
I want to be able to defend it and get the heck out of here. I had
my first hypothesis rejected – at least I'm finding out what they
don't want. But in the process, I periodically get behind in daily
studies so I end up burning the midnight oil. I have not written
my folks for two weeks – I guess that's not much consolation.

I was glad to hear that you got off lightly in traffic court. You
must have given that judge one of your 'winks.' I would have
found you not guilty. Better luck next time – maybe you'll get a
younger judge.

I was going to call you tonight but remembered 'homecoming.'
Hope you had a good time. Do you double with Jane? She
sounds like a very nice person. I wonder if I'll get to meet her at
Christmas or some time. I will have to thank her for watching
over my little Sweet Pea. Talking about your friends – do you
ever hear from Karen or anybody we knew this summer? Please
send my regards if you're in contact with them. ('Especially.
. .what's-her-name' downstairs. . .now Sweet Pea, I'm just
kidding!)

I will try to call you Sunday. That is a good idea about
reversing charges. At least you will get one letter a month from
me – when I send money to pay my bill. I do miss talking to
you and being near you … more than you may realize. In my
own blundering way, I love you very much. The ravages of
time have not been very kind to us. I cannot help but wonder
what may have been if we met at another era of our lives -- oh,

oh, best not go any farther. All I wanted to say is that I love
you and respect you with enrapture I never before perceived
possible. Until then . . . Ok?

Miss ya,
Duane

Sunday October 29, 1967

Hi Good-looking,

Man, I've had a messed-up weekend. I have been running
around with these guys I met in the library at Emory
University. We were looking for a place to move into. There
are four of us.... Just got back from talking to you on the
phone. I feel lower than a snake. Loretta, I am a fool thinking
that you would put up with me not writing, and not calling.
I rationalized that maybe you would forget me when I came
down here so I didn't want to make it hard for you. I was
afraid that you felt obligated to me and would feel tied down
and that it would develop into something neither of us would
want. Now I feel that you really have some feelings for me. I am
glad that you called me and chewed me out. I had it coming. I
don't know why I'm so stupid sometimes (sometimes??) I love
you Loretta. I know what love is and what it means to be made
a fool of in the game of love. (I don't like the term 'game' but
can think of no better right now.) When I met you, I was very
prejudiced against love and everything that went with it. But
you and your family have altered those prejudices very much.
I hope I haven't done something to make me lose the most
wonderful thing that has ever happened to me. I only hope that

I can gain the respect and confidence of you and your family. I pray that the mistakes I make are not bad ones and are few and far between. I respect you for having the patience to put up with me and trying to understand me. I am not making very much sense, am I? I am thinking much faster than I can type. All I am trying to say is thank you, for you. I love you very much. I do miss you very much and when I think of you, I feel so inadequate it makes me sick. But these are things I can't bring myself to divulge or talk about on paper. I hope you know what I mean.

Good-lookin, I am gonna run now. I will write tomorrow when I am thinking more clearly. The red ink doesn't mean I'm mad. It means that I still haven't got around to buying a new ribbon for the old machine. I am so piled down with school work that I have let everything else go to _____! I need a haircut so bad it's not funny, (that is the few I have left). I LOVE YOU AND AM WAITING FOR YOU TO LET ME DO SOMETHING ABOUT IT.

xoxxooxo THE NUT,
Dew

Wednesday, Nov. 1, 1967

Dear Loretta,

Just got back from a night class. It's pouring out; coming down in buckets. I have a good rain coat and I still got soaking wet. But I guess it's better than snow – hmm, I don't know!

I got your card. It was a real gas! Thank you very much. (Man, I'm having trouble with this stupid typewriter.) I suppose I'm falling behind on my promise for more letters but I think I'm improving. Next week and the following week I will have finals. Usually, I go into seclusion and am not heard of until the siege is over. If you are still writing, I will try and reciprocate. Thought about calling you tonight but no one has any change – for honkey, anyway.

Oh, have you heard about EOA (Economic Opportunity Agency)? It did not get refunded. I had a talk with the administrator of EOA here and he thought they might lose their funding – that is where I'm getting my fellowship money. He told me not to worry because the school would probably pick up the obligation. It is costing me about $100.00 more a month than I'm getting. I have spent over $125.00 on books that I need for courses that were not available in the library. Meals cost me about $4.00 a day and I don't know where the rest is going – parties, I guess. (funny, funny)

Time is really flying now. Just a month and 15 days and Christmas vacation will be here. Then I'll be back at the grind for a short eight months and hopefully it will be all over. The prospect of getting the MA doesn't look so gloomy right now.

My advisor says the professors think I'm real PhD material – so at least they aren't thinking about flunking me out. But if they think they can con me into more school-housing, they are nuts. I am anxious to get settled in some position, any position, just so I'm settled. I still have dreams about the future but they're not the same old ones I used to have. I have been a pretty lucky kid – I have seen a lot, did a lot, and known some pretty great people. My feet have lost that itchy feeling; different things seem to please me now – hmm, think I'm getting old?

People change, Loretta. So, don't feel bad if you feel yourself changing. You are very beautiful and young and you could shape your life the way you want. But be careful which routes you choose because you can't back up and it is no easy task to change routes. It's hell to regret a part of your life. Yeah, I know!

Don't try to read anything into what I'm saying. Just a bit of philosophy from a guy who loves you very much. I think that guy had better quit while he's ahead.

Good night,
Dew

Sunday, November 5, 1967

Dear Loretta,

Well, I finally ran out of hotel envelopes but I came across some stationery and you know how cheap I can be at times. Yeah, I still haven't got around to buying a new ribbon for the ole machine, so you have to put up with the red ink.

It has been a hell-of-a week. I told you what happened to me over the phone. On top of it all I have a major exam in Statistics tomorrow. It's the only course that is giving me trouble. I can't keep all the formulas straight. I will be up all night – that is for sure.

Please tell me how much your phone bill has been. I want to reimburse you. Don't even think about paying for it yourself – that would be an insult.

Loretta – I have been in the library all day and am all tied up with school work. As a result, I just can't think of anything real nice to say to you. I am looking forward to seeing you at Christmas – maybe we can get to understand one another a little better so that we won't be frustrated by all the misunderstanding that has seemed to creep in between us.

Please give my regards to everyone – tell them I am very happy down here and am enjoying every minute of it. Ha-Ha! Really, it's not so bad. Time is going fast and I feel that I might make it. Mid-terms are the week after next – so don't be surprised if all things point at me being dead – I usually die at test times! But I hope that I don't neglect to keep you posted – I know now how it feels not to get any letters. It has been a week – okay Sweet Pea, I give. You win – start writing again, alright.

This is gonna be a shorty. Gotta get started on Statistics.

I miss ya. Nothing has changed with me...you know that. Love ya much.

As always,
Dew

10

Time To Move Out

Early Thursday evening, I leave the library entering into a truly gorgeous Georgia night. I've missed Ware Hall's cafeteria service hours but had wanted to get enough references to complete a term paper and figured I'd get a hamburger at the corner hangout on my way home. It is a combination drugstore and lunch counter that has pretty good hamburgers with or without French fries available at a very decent price. There's a crowd just outside the doorway. The hair on the back of my neck stands on end when I see a guy holding and trying to apply a tourniquet to his arm—there's about a five-inch cut on his forearm. Then I notice the other guy, he has an even larger slash on his forehead just above his left eye. Its pumping blood like a fire hydrant, his face is covered with blood. I hesitate for a moment deciding whether I should volunteer to get help. I'm reminded of the color of my skin and realize that my help will not be received well. In the distance, I hear the shrill of a siren penetrating the quiet of the evening. "Help is on the way," I shout and hastily make my exit. When these guys fight, it is not with fists but rather with knives and guns and it's usually sudden, swift, and permanent. There goes my hamburger dinner. I think it's probably best to get some peanuts from the dayroom vending machine.

The weekend is not peaches and cream either. At about 4:00 a.m. on Sunday morning, someone keeps knocking on my door. The knock is loud and steady, not like my *ghost visitations*. I get up to see what the guy wants.

He insists that I am in his room. He is obviously pie-eyed drunk and I am getting nowhere trying to convince him he has the wrong floor. Before security shows up, the whole dorm is out in the hallway lobby. Everyone seems to be enjoying the fracas and half the hallway onlookers are goading the drunk on to demand his room. When security leads the guy away in handcuffs, and the hallway clears, I decide to escape while I still can. My experience of living in the dorm is over!

I think I am the first in the serving line for breakfast in the dorm cafeteria. I have a table to myself and just finished my hotcakes and eggs, when a young lady I recognize from the administration typing pool stops by my table. She informs me, "Dr. McDaniels wants you to drop by sooner than later."

I timidly ask, "Does this have anything to do with last night?"

She shakes her head and responds, "No, you are not in trouble for that but Dr. McDaniels has heard about it."

I quickly finish my coffee and nervously head to Dr. McDaniel's office wondering what's up.

When I arrive, Dr. McDaniels motions for me to have a seat. I am relieved to hear that he wants to discuss my field assignment. He asks, "You don't have a car here, correct?"

I state, "No, sir."

"That's what I thought, let me give you a ride this afternoon since the earlier bus has left and it's unlikely that you'll be able to make the later bus schedule."

As we travel to the Atlanta Employment Evaluation & Service Center, I learn as part of my fellowship I will need to work sixteen hours a week. Upon arrival, he introduces me to the staff (about seventy percent white and thirty percent colored). They explain what the center does and that the

DUANE AND LORETTA JOHNSON

people they evaluate for rehabilitation are Atlanta residents that have been unemployed for six months or more. When Dr. McDaniels tells the staff that I'm the only white student in the dorm they are surprised and seem unsure if they should be in awe or if they should be disgusted.

Bill, the center's supervisor, invites me to dinner in an effort to get to know me better. At dinner he explains, "We evaluate the residents using psychological, medical, and aptitude tests. A team that includes a psychologist, a social worker, and a representative of a manpower team is assigned to each applicant. I would like you to join each team and assess the effectiveness of the various approaches." The more we talk, the more he shares about the operation and the problems that he deals with on a daily basis. He indicates, "I am anxious for you to start so that you can assist with improving our staff." Meanwhile, I hope that his expectations are attainable since I will be in training.

I express concern about getting to work on a timely basis, especially after the horrific traffic congestion on the way over. He responds, "Oh yes, we have some of the worst traffic in the nation."

All I can think is, *Oh, great!*

He offers, "Why don't you get a car and an apartment near the center?"

I counter, "That sounds reasonable but I have no idea of where to go for a car and I have real budget concerns if I can even afford an apartment nearby."

He inquires, "What are you used to driving?"

"I've always had sports-like cars. My last car, which I sold when I found out about the fellowship, was a 1967 Corvette."

Bill says, "My neighbor is a sales manager at an MG dealership. He's also lived in the neighborhood all his life and should be able to help you focus on an affordable place to live."

After dinner we drive to the dealership and he introduces me to his friend and neighbor, then announces, "Duane is in need of transportation."

The sales manager asks me, "What kind of transportation are you accustomed to driving?"

Bill responds for me, "He sold a 1967 Corvette just before coming to Atlanta."

"We don't have any Corvettes currently—but I have other cars available. I have some MGs that were just off-loaded from England. Will you be paying cash?"

"No sir, I had to use most of the money from the Corvette to pay for books, my plane ticket, and other expenses."

The sales manager inquires, "How much do you have to put down, so we can calculate a loan amount?"

I stutter, hmm … umm, when Bill intervenes, "He is one of our team members and is probably looking to finance the entire cost."

The sales manager then assesses my credit as well as my parent's credit. "Why don't you and Bill take a look at our inventory to see what interests you."

I take a black MG GT with a black interior for a test drive and we finalize the negotiation and financial paperwork.

Bill congratulates me and says, "We should look around for a place for you to live and put some miles on your new car." We return to his office and scan the local newspaper ads; he then gets on the telephone to a realtor for rental properties. "We need a single-bed rental with no frills that is close to the Atlanta Employment Evaluation & Service Center at 2455 Abner Place N.W." He comes up with a list of places, most of which are out of my budget.

I spend the next three days looking at "for rent" places, focusing on the lowest-priced ones. I locate a place that was a horse barn, which was converted to a garage and finally to an apartment. It has an electric stove, refrigerator, and a table for my typewriter but won't be available until the landlady cleans it up.

So, for now it's back to the dorm and time to work on more term papers!

Monday, November 6, 1967

Dear Sweet Cheeks,

Man, do I feel bad about that miserable letter I sent yesterday. I was really 'down' and had nothing nice to say – really would have been better off not writing at all but I knew I was falling behind in my correspondence. Then today I get this scrumptious bit of mail from you. Loretta, I don't know how you put up with me. I just hope it will all work out in the end.

I just got back from blowing a big test in Statistics. It was a bitch! He came off the wall with crap I never heard of. I had everything down pat that was covered in class and assigned readings but he managed to dig up some computations that looked like they were in Russian. Oh well, I was not worse off than anybody else – if that is any consolation.

In defense of Dr. Conyers, the test and grading computations may have been a result of an incident just prior to the test. Dr. Conyers had arrived a bit late after the starting bell had rung. He immediately started putting up a problem on the blackboard. He was not quite finished when I raised my hand. As in the past, I was among the first to raise a hand to request my solution to the problem. He turned to me and said, "How would you know the solution unless the problem is completely spelled out?"

With my hand held high, I say, "It's not that. It's the man in front of me. His coat in on fire." Dr. Conyers wheeled around to look at the source.

At the same time, a female co-ed screamed, "Oh my God! He is on fire."

Conyers first statement was, "Everyone knows you can't smoke in class," scolding Bruce as he jumped out of his seat and tried to beat out the fire coming out of his corduroy jacket. The flame wasn't daunted by his efforts so he proceeded to run out of class and into the hallway. Conyers said to the class, "Now what in the world was that all about?"

A few moments later, Bruce came back into the room holding his jacket. The fire now extinguished but a large burnt hole replaced the pocket on his left side. He explained to Dr. Conyers, "I wasn't smoking in class, I had put a pipe in my pocket. Obviously, the pipe embers were still hot and caught fire to my coat." Conyers motions his hand to stop.

"That's enough! Everyone should know you shouldn't smoke or have materials from smoking in the class. With that show, class is dismissed. The next time we meet, there will be a test for everyone," as he walked out of the room shaking his head.

After class Bruce indicated that he was very worried what his wife would say as she had made him the jacket and was quite proud of her sewing skills!

I'm starting to work on Methods and Research tonight. I guess it is part of grad school to test you on material existing about the subject matter regardless of what is covered in class. So, you know what that means – lots of reading and prayers. Prayers that you are covering material pertinent to the test.

Enough of my griping about school. The weather is still great. Real fall weather. It is just cool enough to wear a sweater and maybe a light coat at night. Everyone from down here is running around freezing – talking about hoping that they close school because it's so cold. I was informed that in the event that it snows school will be closed for sure – a standing practice. What do you think about that, Miss Montana? Skiing – most of them have never heard of it, at least not 'snow skiing.'

How's your hangover? Hope the Bobcats beat the big bad Grizzlies. You will have to fill me in on the 'haps' – who did you go out with, where did you go, what did you do, blah-blah?

You asked me what I plan on doing when I get out of school. Well, that depends upon if I get the MA or not. The placement bureau at this school is unbelievable. I have an interview tomorrow with Georgia State Employment Services and one next week with the Atomic Energy Commission. They just come and inform you that this or that company wants to interview you and if you are not interested, you have to cancel the appointment. These are my first two – I think I will go to them just to find out what it is like. And no, Sweet Pea, I'm not planning on going on a year's vacation after I get out. You know I'm too money hungry for that – maybe a couple of months. Actually, I've never had it so good. I worked eight hours a day when I was going to under-graduate school and this makes a bit of difference. You should try and get an application to teach here in Atlanta. The living standard is high and the surrounding country is beautiful. Plus, it is centrally located near – to New Orleans, New York, Wash., D.C. the whole bit. But that is for you to decide. You probably want to teach in Fort Benton or Havre – not that there's anything wrong with that. But if you do go to a small town, it will be hard for me to be located near to you. In my field the big money is in the city. Even if I teach college, most are located in bigger aggregates of population. But really, it's too soon for me to say. The truth is, if I thought that you would put up with me, I would take a job washing dishes just to be near you. (I hope I haven't spooked you with all that jazz about money-money-money. It helps but there is a lot more to being happy and contented. The latter two are my prime objectives regardless of what I do.)

Man – I didn't know I could be so long winded. I suppose I'll have to put an extra five-cent stamp on this one. The ole pony will get a workout tomorrow – hope he makes it. You will have to rest your eyes after you get through this one. By the way, how are your eyes? I know you went to a doctor – did he say anything about you having to wear regular glasses? I (know-it-all) really think it wouldn't hurt – at least in your room when you are reading and stuff! Do you remember how self-conscious I used to be about wearing mine? Well, now I sleep with them on. I got tired of putting them on and taking them off.

How many days? I'm too busy to look at a calendar. I really am excited to see you again. I wouldn't have made it this far without you. I got all sorts of things I want to wisper (sic) to you – good things. (Damned, if I haven't misspelled about every other word in this letter! And I wanted to be cool talking about WHISPERING and all, what a retard I'm getting to be.) Do you think you can do anything for me, Miss Guidance Counselor? How about booking me for about the 16th of December – leave the hours open, okay?

Yeah, I do, you know I do. That will never change I don't care how deranged my mind gets. I still haven't met one to compare you with…not even a close comparison, white or black. I don't know if I should give up looking or what. What do you think?

I'm not going to say any more about my typing…if you don't.

xoxoxoxoxoxoxoxoxoxoxoxoxo Now you owe me!

Love ya,

Friday, November 10, 1967

Dear Loretta,

Hi kid! What's happening? I called tonight and your roommate said that you had gone home for the weekend. I hope you made it okay and that you had a real good time. Hope you said 'hello' to everyone for me. Do you get any more feedback from your parents concerning me? I would sure like to know what they say.

I guess I have no room to complain but do you know that the last letter I received was the 'stinky' one. That has been a week – hmmm, I suppose you're getting even with me. Well you win! How about a line, even if you are mad, okay? I guess everyone has given up on me. My folks haven't written for two weeks

– but then I haven't sent them a letter for ages. But I call them about every week so don't accuse me of being 'inconsiderate.' Maybe I am.

I got my permanent field placement. I have to work 16 hours a week at the Atlanta Employment Evaluation & Service Center. It is a very unique place. They take hard-core unemployed and give them psychological, medical and aptitude tests. Then they are assigned a team which consists of a psychologist, a social worker, and a representative from a manpower team. They evaluate the person and start a program of "rehabilitation." Really, they are the most total approach I have ever seen or read about. I have been assigned to evaluate the teams of which there are 16. My thoughts are that I would like to utilize the collection of data for my thesis. I was given a private office and have access to all the files and was very impressed with the way everybody seemed scared to death of me. I don't think my evaluation is going to carry much weight because it is part of my training – that of evaluating programs – and it is my first but they don't know this, I guess. The supervisor took me out to dinner and was telling me all about the operation, the problems, etc., and he would apologize for this department and assured me that he was anxious to get my report so he could improve procedures. The thing will probably be the death of me because I used Tuesday and Thursday to study and write term papers. I still have about 23 to do, that includes three major ones. If you still want, I'll bring a couple home for you to type – then you'll be more compassionate towards your Sweet Pea. My goal is still to have them all done before Christmas so I can relax when I get home. I have three – oops four mid-terms left.

Two are on Friday, two hours apart – damn! Well I won't go into that – it just gets me to worrying.

I now have decided to get a studio apartment close to where my field placement is. The area looks half-way nice and I was informed, there are apartments available. Everybody is awe stricken when they find out I'm still alive. I informed my advisor that I planned to move off campus and he reacted really funny – but agreed that it would probably be a good idea. Tonight, at supper a bunch of the younger guys said they were going out 'honkey hunting' – just as long as they don't start poaching on the game reserve. I'm okay. I have learned a lot about tactics used by the militants. I will have to tell you all about it over a pizza and beer.

Loretta…please put up with my writing habits this coming week. I will try to call some night, okay. I've got to get on the books. Essay tests here are a bitch! You have to document your arguments with an explanation of the theory, the author, and the works. It is tough enough to take a stand on the issues presented, let alone to know enough about it to know who has said what about it. I got a test back last week – an 85, my worst to date. I had taken the position that Durkheim had on a discussion on deviant behavior. The professor had marked – "a very good interpretation of the question. The use of Durkheim was a sound approach; however, my friend T. Parsons furnishes a more contemporary argument. I will give you a 100 but must deduct 30 off of Durkheim's argument. Score 85 – I think you should share Durkheim's failure. Be more careful who you team with on these joint efforts" – Now how do you like that for a criticism. I don't know if he was being funny or if he seriously 'shot me down.' Trying to figure out some of these profs is something else. I've never read Parsons so how could I use him. Well, I know that is no excuse.

Kid, I'm going to call it – 30 – for tonight. Take care. Yeah, you know I do!

xoxoxoxxooxoxox I'm way ahead of you.

Always,
Dew

Saturday, November 25, 1967

Dear Loretta;

Hi kid! How was your Thanksgiving holiday? Hope you and Jane had a good time. Also hope Jane is feeling better.

My weekend was not exactly dull. I had a big row with one of the guys in the dorm. He came in drunk about 4:00 A.M. and kept knocking on my door. So, I got up to see what the hell he wanted and he insisted that I had the wrong room. Man, I blew my cools…and before it was all over the whole dorm was out in the hallway. Well, nothing became of it except that I have now decided to get the hell out of here while the getting is good.

I also, observed a night of some violence on Thursday night while coming out of the library. Once again, two guys had been fighting and one had a cut on the arm while the other one fared worse than that with a six-inch cut on his forehead. It was above his eye and was bleeding profusely. I don't stick around as I never know how they will feel about me.

A couple days ago I bought a 1967 MG GT. It is black with a black interior and looks really good. It cost $3498.00. I negotiated them down to $3100.00 but by the time I paid the sales tax and bought the license it was back up to $3500.00. The rest of the day I spent looking for apartments – with limited luck. But you can rest assured by the end of this week, I will be in an apartment of my own. I am kinda mad at myself because I blew the whole weekend. I was going to get two term papers out but that looks impossible now. And I went and caught a cold. Something must be wrong with me because I've had three colds this year – one in Havre, another when I first got here and this damn thing. This is very unusual for me because I usually never even get a sniffle – must be old age.

Now I'm hoping for good weather at Christmas. Then I'll drive home and have a 'good' car to go skiing in. Really, I just want you to see it and drive it and tell me what you think. It is really a true sports car. Look around and see if you can spot a '67 around…that's a series 'T.' The best you know.

Did I tell you that I got a perfect paper in "The Sociology of the Family?" The teacher said I had more than he expected and was very well expressed. It was the only A. Kid, things like that are what keeps me going besides the fact that I know I must achieve something great to deserve you.

By the way…I know I bugged you the last time I called but I didn't think I made you mad enough to quit writing. You said you were gonna send me a card…hmm…you didn't goof and send it to Rastus, did you? I will call you as soon as I get settled and give you my new address. Until then, you can send all cards and letters to the same ole one but don't try to call me at the dorm; this is my last night here, I hope.

Well, not many days left till Christmas. If I drive, I will skip Friday classes and leave Thursday morning. Hope to make it to Montana in three days, if the weather isn't bad. I will still pick up my plane ticket in case Montana looks too rough to drive. I think I can cash in an unused ticket. I will find out – Sweetie, take good care of yourself and hang tough! I'm as good as on my way home now. Then you can tell me where to go...but I'll still love you.

Yours Forever,
Duane

Tuesday, November 28, 1967

Hi Good-looking;

Just got back from my field placement. It took me three hours to get 'home.' Freeway was tied up really bad and then I missed my turn-off. So, I got off and had something to eat and gave it another try about an hour later. You can't believe the traffic here at rush hours. I've been around, (I thought) San Francisco, Los Angeles, Seattle and this has got to be the worst! My car is running pretty well but it is nothing like the 'Vette' – I am getting tired of buying cars and getting them running right and then turning around and buying another. After I graduate, I think I will buy ...I don't know what, but whatever, I'm gonna run it till the wheels fall off.

I am way behind in my term papers. I just hope I can make up for it at Christmas. I was weighing the idea of staying here and getting them done but that would be committing suicide as far as our relationship is concerned – so be looking for me and be ready to do some typing, okay?

It is forecasted to snow here in Atlanta tonight. People say this is one of the coldest winters they have seen. To me, it was like summer except maybe for the rain. It does cool off pretty good at night but no more than it does in Glacier Park in the late summer. I am kinda anxious to see what these people call snow. But I don't think I'll try to drive…these people drive like they're nuts now; I would hate to see them drive on snow or ice.

I am not having much luck finding a place to stay. At least, I cannot find anything in the price range that I have set for myself. As it is now, I think I'll be bankrupt by the time I graduate anyway. How does that grab you? Associating with a pauper!

I really can't get too concerned about anything anymore. I think it's too much school…that is all I care about is if the library will be open, when my tests are, what courses I'll be taking next semester. You know, all the important things in life.

But then I get a letter from you and I'm saved. Loretta, you have got to be the greatest. I love you and I think I always will. It is really too bad for me that we have so many things working against us. No matter how I feel or wish the only thing I will strive to achieve is to see that you are happy. I cannot see how you have put yourself in such a predicament…one that is sure to be frustrating and traumatic no matter which way you turn. Oh, I have been reading about interfaith marriage with

Catholics. They seem to be kinda successful as far as not ending in divorce but as far as happiness is concerned it painted a dim picture. (I don't know why I threw that in).

Man, what a dud I am. All I started out to say is thank you for writing and giving me so much encouragement and look what happened. If I make it through this mess, the first thing I'm gonna do is go see a head shrinker...or maybe go and get good and drunk. Both provide good therapy, don't you think? All B.S. aside...thank you for being you and for being part of my life.

Hey, I have said quite a lot in a very short time. Now I know there are probably misspelled words and some that have been used wrong but don't let that bother you. I think I'm doing really well for a retard.

Hey – how many days? Wish you were here tonight. I am really in the mood to talk to you. I hope I feel this way at Christmas.

Always,
Dew

11

The Test

Still waiting for my apartment to become available, the heavy night air seems lighter on my walk from the classroom toward my dorm. I must admit that I have forged a relationship with several of the brothers in the dorm. They have given me, as a term of endearment, the nickname 'Johnny', which is short for Johnson, I assume. The rain has ended and it seems cooler than usual yet there's also an enlightening warming effect. Midterm tests are over, at least for me.

Leaving the classroom after me, Hector the Greek calls, "Hey Johnny, wait up! Did you lay it on *the Man*?"

"I gave him more sociology than I ever knew I had," I respond.

Hector says, "Let's drop off these books and see if we can't scare up something to drink."

"Good idea." The dorm is quieter than usual as some of the students are still entangled in the confrontation of their midterm exam.

Hector says, "I saw you went up and got more blue books. You must be writing a textbook on sociology."

"I've never written for so long ever in my life!" I drop my stuff off first, then we hurry to Hector's room where his roommate Cy is waiting for us. Cy and I watch as Hector drops his things on his bed and pulls out a twelve-inch butcher knife, which he places in his belt.

Loudly, I ask, "What in the hell is that for?"

"We're going to Turner Street and it's my protection. Everybody knows you have yours. Everyone knows that you got a .357 in your boots. You joining us, Cy?"

"Nah, I'll wait for you guys to get back."

There's too much night life on the street at this hour. As we approach the liquor store, Hector mutters, "Wait right here. You don't need to go in there to stir things up."

When we return to the dorm room, there are three other fellows besides Cy that welcome us. Hector sits on his bed and removes the pint of Four Roses whiskey and reads the label, *Four Roses knows what to put inside a bottle ... the taste to win friends, the flavor to make memories.* He unscrews the cap, takes two or three gulps of the whiskey and passes the bottle to Cy who repeats the ritual. Cy then passes the pint to one of the three guys who says he's not drinking tonight. The other two brothers take turns at the diminishing whiskey bottle and then pass it to me. I wipe the spout with the palm of my hand and take a couple man-size gulps.

"Whoa, did you see that, he took a drink after us like he got the bottle first," proclaims the one guy. The three other guys then announce, "We gotta go."

Hector says, "That leaves the rest for Cy, Johnny, and me."

"Can you believe he actually did that?" We hear a voice from the hall.

"I saw him and I didn't think I'd live to see that day with my own eyes but I refuse to drink after him," says another voice. Shortly after their rowdy rejection, the pint of Four Roses is relieved of its content.

Hector says, "That was good whiskey. I could use some more."

Cy answers saying, "I think I'll pass—it goes straight to my head."

Hector asks, "Johnny, do you have any more scratch?"

"Not much but I'll give you all I got. Let's go visit your friendly clerk." I again wait outside the liquor store as Hector engages the clerk.

I can see him spreading our coins on the counter and there seems to be an intense conversation going on between them about another type of liquor that we could purchase that's similar to the pint of Four Roses.

Hector comes out carrying a brown bag, "Johnny have you ever drank Russian Vanya? The clerk says it gives the same kick."

Whoa, I hope I can handle more, I mutter to myself. When we return to Hector's room, he and I are alone and wage war with the Russian drink. When the bottle is empty, I stagger to my room.

When I wake up the next morning my head is pounding and I'm enticed by the smell of cafeteria coffee and eggs. After I look at myself in the hallway mirror, I decide to go back to the room for my shades. I slowly walk to my morning class wondering how Hector is feeling.

As I enter the classroom, the silent treatment is broken with questions like, "What did you do with Hector? He's not here this morning. He will be happy to pass the celebrity of being the last man standing on to you," they exclaim.

Waiting for the test grades to be posted, a couple guys explain to the class what took place last night, which is startling to all. One of the lady students says aloud, "Johnny will pass two tests--acceptable as one of the members of the black community and the test that we took in class."

"Yes, he will," chimes in another.

Sunday November 19, 1967

Dear Loretta;

It's midnight and I'm just getting out of bed. When I finished my last midterm test, I went and got a hamburger and hit the sack. I didn't wake up for 22 hours. Can you believe it? I got up, took a shower, went to chow, and went back to bed. I blew the whole weekend. I hope you didn't wait around for me to call.

The midterms went pretty well. I know I passed but I don't think there is much chance to get an A. As you probably know, a C in grad school is the same as flunking. So, you really have to be on your toes. In all the courses except Statistics I had essay tests. My arm was actually numb when I finished. I have never written so much at one time in my life.

Loretta, I'm really looking forward to having that picture of you. And if it isn't ready for Christmas, I'll wait. And don't you be worrying about getting me anything for Christmas. All I want is to be with you and to get out and see the ole town. I'm afraid that I will have to bring home some work. I still have term papers to get out. I thought I would have them done by Christmas but they keep piling additional work on so that is almost out of the question now. But we'll see a lot of each other regardless, I hope. We've got to go skiing, so take care of your legs – I don't want any excuses.

Guess you noticed I have finally gotten a new ribbon for the machine. It hasn't helped my typing though.

The weather here is getting pretty cold. It is supposed to go down to 32 degrees tonight. And that's cold here, kid. I haven't got much to report. I will try and knock out a couple more this week – at least a couple before Christmas vacation. I got to get busy on an assignment for Monday in Statistics. Take care, and I'll be seeing you at 10:30 on the 16th.

I know I must have more to say but I feel wasted.

Love,
Duane

Tuesday, November 21, 1967

Hi Loretta;

How's things? Say you have really been sending those cards and letters in, haven't you? Thanks kid. I know it's just as hard for you to find time to write as it is for me. Every word I get from you encourages and gives me a feeling that there is still reason to 'fight on.' You are great to take the trouble. I just wish I could jump in the ole car and run up to see you. Those few times we had together will always be remembered with nostalgia for me. (Now don't let Jane see that word nostalgis (sic) –it is probably spelled wrong and means some stupid thing I didn't mean.) What I mean is…hmm…what do I mean. I think I am trying to say… I love you. Now, you can let anyone see that.

Midterms were a bitch, but I made it. I still feel wasted…can't get started back on the daily grind.

Oh, I looked into flights out of here sooner. No luck! But they put me on standby for Thursday and Friday. They advised me against it unless I can get flight clearance all the way to Great

Falls. I could end up getting stuck in Denver or St. Louis...and with my luck that's what would happen.

Nothing new. Same old bull. Not even any excitement – no one has shot each other, no one has broken into my room lately, etc., so am getting bored. Maybe I could start a race riot.

Well, I'll wait until Christmas to seek excitement. In my old age I should really try to avoid too much excitement...like a good-looking girl meeting me at the airport. What do you think?

I should have double-spaced this thing. I have absolutely nothing to write.

Yeah, you know I do.

Love ya,
Dew

Sorry about this letter! I'm just not with it tonight. I need you to perk me up.

12

Chased Out By The Rats

It's my second day in my new apartment, still not feeling like home. While sitting at my new study table in what I refer to as the "Bennett Apartment," I peruse the map for the route from my new College Park apartment to the Atlanta Employment Evaluation & Service Center. I'm feeling quite proud of myself, considering the size of this city, for finding my way around. I did take the wrong exit one time and had to backtrack across a number of railroad tracks in order to navigate the city center. My worst driving challenge, to date, was three hours to travel from the center back to Ware Hall because the freeway was backed up with bumper-to-bumper traffic. I eventually got off and had something to eat and then tried again with a full stomach an hour later. Traffic congestion on the Atlanta Connector is a lot different from any traffic I experienced in the Northwest and definitely in Great Falls.

I am startled by a knock on my door. It's Mrs. Bennett who I invite in as she seems anxious to enter and discuss the apartment rules. With the authority of a landlady, she says, "There will be no alcohol, no visitors after dark, no women at any time, and you must keep the place neat and tidy."

I look around and admit to myself that she's done a darn good job of cleaning the former barn/garage which is now my apartment. I quickly respond, "Mrs. Bennett, I understand your rules. You have nothing to worry about since as a graduate student my main focus is my education. I am very satisfied to be living in this apartment while getting my degree."

Mrs. Bennett is quick to confront me about the school I'm attending. She realizes it is an all-black university and quickly accepts that. What seems to concern her more is my area of study, as she peruses my textbooks. She bows her head and repeatedly says, "Mr. Johnson, don't you know that socialism and communism can cause you a lot of problems?"

I correct her, saying, "It is sociology and not socialism. I assure you that sociology can be a useful weapon against the introduction of communism into the United States."

She acknowledges my opinion but reiterates the need to keep my place neat and clean as she departs.

I get up and assess the contents of my refrigerator. I have half-a-dozen eggs, six grapefruits, and six cans of Pepsi which will sustain me for two days' worth of my diet. On Friday, I go to a Burger Master for that day's special. While the Burger Master's Friday special sets me back $1.75, it is a welcome change from my daily diet. I notice that there's still one-third of a pecan pie that will disappear before I head out. While taken aback by Mrs. Bennett's rules and misunderstandings about today's societies, I don't ever turn down the Sunday pecan pie that she leaves for me on her way to her church.

The pecan pies are in payment for the car rides I will give her to downtown College Park. Although I don't fully understand why riding the bus isn't safe. She's tried to explain, "You never know where a colored person sat before you."

I tried to tell her, "Mrs. Bennett, you can sit in a row by yourself or with another white person."

But according to Mrs. Bennett, you are likely to come down with consumption if you sit in a seat that a colored person sat in previously.

As I held my tongue she uttered, "Mr. Johnson, don't you know consumption is a widespread disease among colored folks? Don't you know what that means?"

Sometimes, I'm not sure how I feel about these Southern whites' mores of the time.

* * *

It's now early December and I complain to Mrs. Bennett, "At times, the noise from the rats in the ceiling and walls has caused me to stop studying and writing term papers. If that is not enough," I bravely continue, "I even saw one poke his head out from the sheetrock."

She quickly promises professional help in reining in the rats.

Within a day or so after our discussion, she appears with two men dressed in coveralls with green logos that read RAT PAC DIMMERS. After inspecting the premises and the yard, they return to where I'm standing with Mrs. Bennett.

"There's a passel of rats in and around your apartment," the taller, older gentleman states matter- of-factly. "We can do them in but no one can be living on the premises during this time."

"How long?" I ask eagerly.

"Minimum of two weeks and a maximum of three weeks," the other man adds.

"I can't charge Mr. Johnson rent if he can't live in the apartment," Mrs. Bennett mutters to herself.

"Understood, but we don't want to kill him in the process," the older gentleman wisely states.

To me, this is my license to get a round trip ticket home to Great Falls, returning in fourteen days. I just need to check if the department head at school has made a decision as to whether we can leave or will have to stay and work at the Atlanta Employment Evaluation & Service Center.

Loretta has been understanding about the fact that I may not get home for Christmas. I don't think she shares my worries regarding our misunderstandings and my concern for our fragile relationship. I fear a breakup if we are not able to rekindle our love.

I decide to head for the center hoping that I can meet with Miss White, the Director. As I drive to the center, I am jubilant just thinking about the possibility of going home for Christmas. Upon my arrival, I see Miss White is in her office and I approach her secretary.

Miss White greets me warmly and asks, "What brings you in, Duane?"

After greeting her, I ask, "Do you know yet if the center will be open during the Christmas and New Year's holiday?"

She responds, "I was just getting ready to put up a memo saying that we will be closed during the holidays." She asks, "Will you be staying in town?"

Eagerly, I say, "No, I am being chased out of my apartment by rats!"

She looks puzzled but leaves her comments unsaid.

Sunday, December 3, 1967

Hi Loretta,

It sure was good to talk to you Friday night. I think you must be the greatest person alive to understand the way you did about all the problems arising down here. I hope to know by Wednesday what the scoop is.

I didn't get a chance to pick up a money order yesterday but will get one tomorrow morning and send it airmail. I hope you get it in time to pay the phone bill before you leave on vacation. And I hope $50 is enough. I am not planning on putting in a phone here because I don't want anybody down here finding where I live or calling me. I want to isolate myself from the school as much as possible...for reasons you already know.

I called home yesterday and my folks were upset at the idea that I might not be home for Christmas. My Mother was especially upset. She had a lot of things planned and now she doesn't know what to go ahead and do. I guess I have messed up everybody's plans. The thing that bothers me is I hope nobody blames me. Right now, it is beyond my control.

Yesterday and today, I have really been homesick. The weather here has been dreary, like it could snow, and the radio has been playing Christmas songs...all combined have tended to make me feel pangs of nostalgia. If I don't get to go home for Christmas, it just won't be much of a Christmas for me at all... oh blah. I must be getting too sentimental for my old age.

My Mom told me that Frank Hayes had been down and visited with her. The program up in Havre has gone to pot, I guess. They are closing it down. He was going to try to get a job as a counselor with the State Employment Office in Great Falls. I wish him luck. He was actually a very nice guy.

How have you and Jane been doing? I hope you kids are having a good time and don't get bogged down. I sure wish that some time we all could get together and spend a weekend skiing or something. Do you think that would be fun? How about it, would you save a little time for your old flame?

132

You always accuse me of being cold and not writing anything that would seem to express my devotion to you. Well right now, I am exploding with love for you but, again, it doesn't seem right to be revealing such intimate thoughts to an ole typewriter. This stupid thing just doesn't seem to care one way or another. So, such moods will have to wait...for a time when we can be together, when I can touch you and reassure you that the things, I say are good. Now, more than ever, I am concerned whether I will ever get that chance. But, if it will help, I do care, and I do love you – very much. All I can ask you is to 'hang tough.'

Forever,
Dew

December 6, 1967

Dear Loretta;

Today I received my first letter at my new address. Now this place really feels like home. I have been running around like a mad Russian, trying to get a money order and insurance for my car.

Loretta, Loretta, Loretta, I don't know what I meant by all that crap about mixed marriages. I think I was just trying to show off my schooling. I hope it didn't start you to wondering what kind of a nut I am...besides you should know that by now. As far as the church is concerned, I hope you know how I feel about that. I feel a sincere obligation to do what is right in the eyes of the church and more important what you thought

133

was right. But that is a bridge not even in sight just now, so we will procrastinate.

We still haven't got word from the department head about our holiday status. I think they are trying to avoid the issue. But I am still gonna try and make it home, if only for a couple days. I am afraid that your folks would be a little apprehensive about you coming down here. But it was a good idea and if something happens that I can't make it I will get ahold of you immediately.

Today, I was picked up by the police for not having a license on the car. They told me they usually imprison and impound the car. But I went to the station and called the dealer who had promised to pick up the license and mail them to me. He had the license in an hour so they let me go. What next?

I must go now. I have a class from the Department Head so maybe tonight's the night. I will call if we do get word.

Good luck on exams! Sorry about my letters – short and far between but I hope I can make it up to you...soon.

Forever,
Dew

13

Decision: Stay Or Leave

I return from Montana more in love with Loretta than ever and force myself to postpone dreaming about our future. I must finish my term papers and prepare for finals, which are fast approaching. Dreading seeing the department head, Dr. Cothran, who never actually gave a decision regarding our Christmas vacation, I enter his meeting room, which consists only of fellowship recipients. He sternly proclaims to all of us, "I am taken aback that you are now in charge and can determine your own holidays!" I slink down into my chair wondering what is yet to come. As Cothran moves on, I quietly say to myself, *thank goodness, I met with Miss White at the Center and confirmed they would be closed during the Christmas holidays.*

Cothran continues, "Since this is a new program, I have been meeting with representatives of the Federal Government regarding any additional requirements of the program. In addition to the sixteen hours a week that you are required to put in at agencies like the Atlanta Employment Evaluation & Service Center, the Federal Government has said that you *will not* receive your MA degree upon completion of your coursework in August."

"What now?" Bruce, one of the other white recipients of the fellowship, exclaims.

Cothran explains, "Because you have been attending graduate school on the government's money, they are telling us that all fellowship recipients will have to fulfill another obligation prior to receiving your degrees."

"Why are we just hearing this now?" I ask, trying to keep from screaming.

Dr. Cothran states harshly, "You have been receiving a great deal of money for tuition, fees, room and board, in addition to a monthly stipend! It has been determined that you will also need to spend one year working for an agency that focuses on poverty. You can either find an agency on your own or we will place you at one in the Atlanta area."

"Is this final or will this change as well?" Bruce questions in an unpleasant tone.

"This is final and if there are no further questions, you are free to leave."

Fuming, I return to my car and drive to my apartment. As I enter my abode, I see my typewriter and am reminded that there is a term paper awaiting me. Enjoying my Christmas vacation and spending a dazzling time with Loretta, I had failed to finish writing it. My preference at this moment is to buy a diamond ring for Loretta, get behind the wheel of the ole MG GT and head northwest until I reach Montana. I come to my senses and realize I want good grades, even if I decide to leave at the end of the semester and finish my master's degree elsewhere.

As I turn on my radio, I hear the weather report—the temperature will go down to five degrees above zero tonight. After the snow, ice, and 35 below temperatures in Montana, this is nothing. The forecaster recommends that everyone add antifreeze to their cars, stay home, and *avoid* driving on the slick roads.

The knock on the door in the middle of the evening startles me, but I realize it can only be Mrs. Bennett, so I get up and let her in. She is wearing a brown coat, covered by an orange parka, red scarf, and black mittens. It looks as though she just left the Goodwill store and is heading for the Arctic.

"Oh, Mr. Johnson, I saw your light on and thought I should check to see if you'd like a heating pad because of the dreadful cold temperatures. I'm terribly sorry that you have to deal with such frigid weather."

"Thanks, but I will be fine. You remember that I am from Montana, right?"

"Very well, good night now. Will you be staying home tomorrow?"

"No, I will be going to class as usual," I explain sincerely. Little did I know that as a result of receiving half an inch of snow overnight, the freeways are blocked and shut down. All schools, stores, and government offices are closed. It's as if they just received 4 feet!

At 3:00 a.m. on Thursday, I complete my last term paper, which weighs in as an eighty-four-page thesis-like document! I then begin studying for finals. My current grade in Advanced Statistics is a low B as a result of the professor's hated intrusion of honkies into the bastion of higher learning in the South. He refers to Atlanta University as the Black Harvard of the South. A clear example of reverse prejudice is apparent. On my last test I had two wrong answers and received a C+ while the guy next to me got a B+ with five wrong answers. I foolishly ask Dr. Conyers, "What is your reasoning?"

He states very adamantly, "I never take anything away from anybody. Two wrong is a C and if I think you need a little help; I give additional points. That's my business."

I hesitate and don't respond since I'll need a good background in advanced statistics to conduct research and, of course, that's where the money is.

My only good news from today's meeting with fellowship recipients is that the one-year obligation is now a nine-month obligation. It seems as though they can't make up their minds. The rest of the meeting with the department head doesn't go well. There are three of us that are planning to drop out of the program at the end of this term. When we advise Cothran of our intentions, he loses his cool. "You are being unfair to the school and the program." He screams, "Do what you want, none of you are capable students anyway! We knew that we would have dropouts."

The three of us have the highest grades in all of our classes so he should dream up a better justification, I want to say.

During my Friday night phone call with Loretta, I tell her, "Unless something very unusual comes up, I will be dropping out of the program here at the end of this semester."

* * *

I continue to push forward with my studies, regardless of my decision to possibly leave. I'm delighted when I receive my thesis proposal back from my first reader who says my proposal is good and well written. Dr. McDaniels is a good guy and does not seem to be displaying any prejudice toward me. The second reader Dr. Williams, is not as positive with his constructive criticism, albeit the entire objective of my thesis will change.

I realize that I should tell my advisor, Dr. Clyde McDaniels, of the possibility that I may drop out. I swing by his office and discover that he is available. As soon as he invites me in, I nervously state, "I want to advise you that I plan to drop out after the final semester exams."

He is visibly shaken and asks, "Why? What's going on?"

I refrain from telling him about my discontent with the program and the nine-month obligation and tell him, "I plan to go back to Montana and marry my girlfriend."

He responds saying, "You are getting your tuition and everything paid for now and it will run $56.00 plus per credit if you start graduate work at a similar place such as Washington State University in Pullman." He continues, "I think for financial reasons you should remain until you have fulfilled your program requirements."

"Thank you Dr. McDaniels, I appreciate your perspective and will consider your advice," I respond.

I then go to my Methods class and receive the results of my eighty-four-page term paper. Dr. Williams has made complimentary comments and gives me the only A in the class! I'm encouraged as this will lead me to my thesis along with the data that I am currently gathering at the Atlanta Employment Evaluation & Service Center.

I finish my last two tests on Friday and Saturday, and am preparing to move on. Loretta is always in my daytime thoughts and now in my dreams, which is unusual for me. I recently read Dr. Martin Luther King wooed his future wife by telling her: "My life without you is like a year without a springtime which comes to give illumination and heat to the atmosphere which has been saturated by the dark cold breeze of winter." While he became one of the greatest orators of our time, my only wish would be to express my love for Loretta in a few poetic words. I shake my head and think to myself; *I need to quit day dreaming and think about getting serious.*

I'm dead broke and need to dust off my printer skills acquired in Great Falls, and work for a few nights at *The Atlanta Journal*, where I make

$35.00 a night as a substitute printer. I am thankful I can work at my choosing rather than full time. Getting off shift at 1:30 a.m. feels very lonely. Dark and empty streets pull at my heartstrings with no one to meet me when I return home.

My third shift ends on Monday. I realize that I don't want to end up working nights as a printer—which is how I'm feeling in my current uncertain state. My thinking is shifting and I call Loretta, "Sweetheart, I hope you won't be upset and will understand my decision is made from my love for you. I realized that if I leave the program here, I'll feel insecure and question if I can give you the kind of life, we both want to share with our family. I've decided before I can ask you to share your life with me, I must persevere and finish the program and receive my MA degree."

"I understand and support your decision," she responds in a mature and loving manner.

I feel relieved and more in love with her than ever.

Thursday, January 4, 1968

Hi Loretta,

Well, here I am, back in Georgia. I have mixed feelings about being back. The weather is really nice (about 60 degrees) and the grass is green…but you aren't here. I miss you more now than ever before. It is hard to settle down to work with you constantly on my mind. But I suppose the initial shock of being separated will dissipate and then I'll have to get to know you all over again. I hope the next time will be final and lasting.

Last night we had a meeting with the head of the department. He made some cutting remarks about students declaring their own holidays but said nothing more about me not working *during the holidays. Then he hit us with a bomb. He explained how this is a new program and that things have just now been ironed out with the government concerning what they wanted from us as recipients of the fellowships. We will be finished with our course studies in August. Then we are obligated to work with an agency that deals with people in poverty for one year and then we get our M.A. The only ones that screamed were the white students and then only two of us. I wouldn't mind working for an agency for a year but it gripes me to no end that we will not receive the degree until this obligation is fulfilled. It means a reduced wage for that year, for one thing, and then it just drags this M.A. bit out. We can solicit our own job or they will place us. If they place us, it will be in the Atlanta area. So...now what? I plan to write Bill Cady at Employment Services in Great Falls and also the poverty program there to see if I can get employment there starting next fall. But if you decide on a place to work, I would naturally solicit employment in close proximity to where that would be...if you like it or not. Your response is a major variable that will decide what I will do.*

Loretta, I want to thank you for the great time I had while home. I was all ready for you to dump the whole affair. What with the mess it appears to be at times...but somehow, I got the feeling that our relationship is workable and could be radiant. Once again, I was impressed with the mature and sensible attitude that you possess. If you feel that you could be happy with a creep such as me, then I pray that you will have patience and give me a chance to be around you so I can give you some of the happiness that I have received from you. If I could grow old seeing you happy and content, then I would feel that I have been rewarded for anything I might be brought to task to do... Oops, getting wordy again. Guess you know by now I'm a little bs'er. What I'm trying to say is that I love you...I need you and all I want is to believe that you want and need me.

I have your picture proudly displayed in the front room where I do most of my studying. I was going to put it by my bed but thought better...I am afraid I wouldn't get any sleep. I have a working agreement with the rats. If they don't mess with you, I won't mess with them.

I still have to get a thank you card for your folks. Loretta, you can be thankful for having a family like you do. They have got to be the greatest people I have had the privilege to meet. I hope that I wasn't 'such of a headache' to them during the holidays. I think I will always remember my stay in Big Sandy this Christmas. Thank you for inviting me up.

I just heard that postage on first class mail is going up six cents. Wow...I think I would come out ahead if I moved to Bozeman and went on welfare. I really am feeling the pinch from not working. I hope I will adjust soon because I have really drained my savings. I have decided to save $100.00 a month while here in school regardless...so if you don't recognize me (I'll probably look like a starved cowboy just off the range) it's because I have been conservative with spending money on clothes and food. I plan to stand on the corner by the First National Bank with my cow hat during rush hours to see if I can pick up a little change. Every little bit counts.

Must get busy on a term paper...the one I was going to do while I was home. Work has really piled up and there is only a week left before everything is due. Then another week before finals...so I might get behind with my letter writing. I hope you will understand, Even, if I quit at the semester, I want good grades so that I can get into another school without problems.

My typing has gone all to hell. I can tell I will have fun typing term papers. My professors are not as understanding as you are when they read my waggery. (I think there is such a word... it means B.S.) Well...got to get busy...and I have such of a headache, too.

Love from your ole cookie man.
Forever yours,
Duane

I can't draw either! But I love you...xoxoxoxxx.

Sunday, January 7, 1968

Hi Good-looking,

Please excuse the paper and the terrible handwriting. I am in the middle of a paper and I don't want to unload the typewriter. Okay? I have really been busy. I was up 'till 4:00 AM writing the last term paper. Naturally, it has turned out to be a bugger, the toughest of the lot! I have 38 pages and haven't covered half the material. Oh, well – I have until Friday to turn it in.

Tomorrow I have a test in Statistics. Haven't even started to study for it. But I think it's the type you can cram and get by – I hope!

It is supposed to get down to 5 degrees above zero here tonight. Everybody is panic stricken. Putting anti-freeze in their cars, etc. My landlady came over and wanted to know if I wanted to use a heating pad. She was apologizing for the weather and acted really concerned. Kind of a joke, huh? What with the weather in Montana!

No word from you yet, Sweet Pea. What's happening? Have you found yourself another cookie? Better shape up or I'll forget your birthday – hear! I saw a nice cowgirl outfit in the Sears catalog I thought would be nice. What size do you take? I take about a 40 and you're bigger than me so I ordered a 44. Hope it fits!

Now that I'm in trouble, I'll be nice. Wish I was there to give you a little smooch and tell you I'm only kidding.

I don't have any stamps so you might not get this letter right away. And the six-cent rate went into effect today. Should have taken time last night, I guess.

How was Jane's Christmas. Hope you two are staying out of trouble – and away from all those college men. Damn, I get jealous just thinking about it. Oh, I found out that I have a nine-month obligation instead of a year. Wish these people in charge would make up their minds. I was explaining my plight to the supervisor at the Employment Center where I work and he asked me what my big hurry to leave was – and so I told him I had this little filly back in Montana who would be graduating in June and if I wasn't around, I was afraid somebody else would slap their brand on her. He said that chances you could get a job with them in the counseling department. I didn't say much – but I think the wages are *pretty good for a girl – about $500 to start. Let me know if you want me to find out more!*

Hmm! Seems I had something else to tell you too! It must have been about how much I think of you or something. Oh – well, nothing important. You already know that.

Got to go study. Be good. I DO!
Duane

P.S. Even if it's a 'Dear John' letter, keep those letters coming! Miss you, xoxoxo!

Sunday, January 14, 1968

Dear Folks,

Hi! Just came back from supper with my landlady. I was out hanging up some sweaters on the line and she was curious about what I was doing—then invited me in for some stew, a hamburger and pecan pie with coffee. It was really good and free. She is a grand old gal. She brought me an electric blanket and is always concerned with how I'm doing. I spend a lot of time listening to her but I guess my time isn't that valuable. Oh, she just brought me a coffee pot and a pecan pie. How do you like that?

Well, the weather has been rather cold down here. It got down to 22 degrees last night. School has been closed and I don't know if it will resume tomorrow or not. It is really crazy. It really feels nice—a little brisk, maybe—but all the stores are closed and the highways are closed. You would think they had just gotten four feet of snow instead of ½ inch.

I am sending $130 home. I would appreciate if Dad would put $50 into United mutual funds. All he has to do is use one of the envelopes that has our name and account number on it and send a check. Put the rest in the bank or use it as you need. I don't want too much here with me because I have a tendency to get a little 'gay' with green stuff in my pocket. I have too much work to do to mess around.

Sorry about all the errors in this here letter but am in a hurry to start studying again. Time is drawing to a close and finals are staring me in the face. Can't get excited about them though. Not happy with the school or the teachers at all. I am very hesitant about continuing with the school down here. Every course is centered around the Negro problems and this has little bearing on what I had intended to do so am not getting what I wanted. Oh well, I can't quit until this semester is done anyway, so have to be concerned a little.

They are in need of printers here in the Atlanta area. If I quit in February, I might stay and work until the weather breaks in the West. Of course, if anyone found out that I went to a "Negro" school, I would not have much of a chance to get work. When I went and paid my union dues, I had to be careful not to talk about school—everybody down here is pretty disgusted with the demands of the Negros and are bitter towards those who take their part. And of course, if it was known that I was integrating a Negro school, I would be lower than cow dung.

Everything in consideration, I am A-Okay. I hope to have time to write all the folks on the coast and thank them for all the cards and letters. It was pretty great to hear from them. Wish they would write more often. Talking about writing—you haven't broken an arm or something have you? Guess I have to do something drastic to shake you up a little—but it's getting so nothing I do shakes you people up—so can't win.

Oh yeah, that reminds me, I am thinking Loretta and I may get married at Easter. I will let you know more when I have time to go into details.

Hang tough,
Your son, Duane

Thursday, January 18, 1968

Dear Loretta,

Just taking a break, thought I'd write you and let you know that I'm alive and still 'together.' I am a little concerned about not hearing from you. Three letters and a card are great...but when you are used to getting a letter every other day or so... guess I was kinda spoiled before Christmas. How about it – what's happening?

I told my advisor yesterday that I was dropping after the semester exams, he flipped. Of course, he wanted to know why. When I told him, he got real interested and started asking about you. He pointed out that I am getting my tuition and all paid for – which would cost about $56 + per credit at Pullman for graduate work. For financial reasons, he thought I should remain at least until I got my requirements in.

Then we went out for a drink – on him. We continued to discuss you and me. He really was concerned when I told him of our problems. Then he took me back to his office and gave me the Bogardus Marital Adjustment Test. Man – our setup scored so low it was unbelievable. What was bad was our difference in religion and age. Bogardus puts a lot of weight on religion and says couples separated by more than four years have a hard time adjusting. Naturally, I scoffed at the test and said it was baloney. But he said I had better think it over and give the relationship a lot of time before any definite steps were taken. (Sounds familiar) ...I was a little negative or harsh when answering test answers. One was if mate ever appeared for a date in rollers, and I said "yes." This really broke McDaniels up. He wondered what kind of girl was that...naturally I explained that you had overslept when I picked you up to go skiing and came to the door in your pajamas and rollers! Then one was about dancing and that I could not stand to dance. That is not really true. But it was stuff like that which had a bearing on the outcome.

Sweet pea, I would feel bad if I lost you but I would feel even worse if I ever caused you to have one maladjusted day in your life. Until I had met you, I didn't think there was any love in me...I would mess around but when things got too close, I would always walk away and forget it. Now I have lost all my coolness and it seems that I can't keep up to you...and you're the one that is running. Maybe, I am getting some of my own medicine. Oh well, we'll see – soon.

I am sort of inhibited tonight because I haven't heard from you for so long. My emotions haven't changed one bit...and you should know that I do love you...so what else needs to be said? Now I'm sounding unaffectionate and cold –damn, I just can't win!

I would feel better if I could hear from you...and once again... tell it like it is.

Sincerely,
Duane E. Johnson

XOXXOOXO – that's all – you little devil! Love ya --

Monday, January 29, 1968

Hi Sweetheart,

Well, finals are over and I'm still alive. Tomorrow we get our grades. I am very curious to know what I got. I think I have two 'A's sacked but don't know for sure. The rest are anybody's guess.

I have been working at the Atlanta Journal since Saturday. I worked Saturday and Sunday and am going to try for a hire tonight. I am subbing and just work one shift at a time. I need the money and it did me good to work in the paper racket again. I don't think I would be satisfied ever, if I had to return to printing for a steady diet. Especially working nights.

Sweetheart, if I don't work tonight, I plan to call you and explain my intentions. I pray that my decision will not upset you and that you will realize that the decision has been made because I love you and want to make you happy – forever.

While I was working, I realized that if something should come up and I didn't return to school and get my M.A.; I would feel very insecure and question my ability to give you the kind of life I know we both want to share. I know that I do not want to be working nights in some newspaper and have you teaching

149

days and not having the time to share our family and love. This caused me to realize that I must persevere and finish graduate school now before I could ask you to give yourself to me. Now I am not so naive to believe that 'absence makes the heart grow fonder,' and I realize that each hour away from you diminishes the chances that you will still be waiting for me when I return. Sweetheart, it is a gamble I must take. It has to be done because I love you and am such a damn idealist that I do not want to have anything less than the best, the very best I can offer for you. I know that I could provide for you as a printer and that chances are pretty good that we could get me through graduate school together, but it would be trying for both of us. And it could very well be an impossibility if we were fortunate to conceive a child. It is for you and ours that this decision has been made.

It might seem that I am once again being cold and too rational, but nothing could be farther from the truth. It (the decision to finish school) has caused me many moments of frustration and downright anxiety. I knew that a decision had to be made and that I had to make it. I wanted to be near you now – right now – to hold you and to smother you with the love I am bursting with…but then I want to keep you forever. I want to always be able to hold you and have you love me in return. I believe that you will agree with me that when it came time to share with our children that we would both feel guilty if we're not able to give them what we both have been fortunate to be given by our parents.

It is my hope that we are destined to share our lives together. I pray that when we are once again together, it will be forever and that time itself will come to a standstill. It is this thought that leads me to believe that we (I know I can but realize that the beauty that you have to offer does not go unwanted by others) will have the fortitude to wait just a few more months.

Honey, if you think I'm all wet, please tell me. Although, I have made this decision, it isn't unchangeable. If I am being too idealistic and inconsiderate (heaven forbid), please share your thoughts with me. All I want in life is to share it happily with you – all other things will be considered a bonus.

I LOVE YOU, MISS NEPIL!

Please don't be upset. If you feel disappointed, talk to Jane (I am hoping she is on my team) and if the decision seems too harsh, please let me know. I will call you and we will have a long talk. Okay, I…well, what I am trying to say now is… honey, please have faith in me and be mine.

Well good-looking, it is time for me to head to work. It is a very lonely feeling walking out of a newspaper at 1:30 in the morning…the streets are deserted…and you feel very alone. There is no one at home waiting for you and no place to go…but I look at it as just another $35.00 in my dowry and someday I will exchange it for you. Fairytales – but it does make me feel like working and saving. Nothing but the best for you – okay, sweetie?

I love you and wish that life wasn't so complicated. I wonder why we couldn't just go to that island you were talking about and live together forever – away from the pettiness of the rest of the world. I would pick coconuts and for a supplement we would have our love.

Loretta, you don't know how much I just want to slip my arms around you and to hold you close to me and to feel the tenderness and warmth of your mouth close to mine. Save all your beautiful kisses for me, please...

Yours for eternity – love and prayers,
Dew

14

Black Power

Stokely Carmichael, the head of the Student Non-Violent Coordinating Committee (SNCC), was the first to popularize the term *black power*. He wanted to change the SNCC's tactics and goals, and challenge the established black leadership for their practice of non-violence. Under his leadership, they became more radical and were known as shock troops of the revolution. As a student of sociology, I agree with the need to develop political and economic self-sufficiency in the black community, but not with violence.

For me, black power has a different definition and originates from my professors at Atlanta University. It can range from blatant reverse prejudice to discreet discrimination. There are times when my advisor, Dr. Clyde McDaniel, or Dr. Samuel Williams, in appreciation of my knowledge and hard work, announce, "Your thesis is providing a unique understanding in the study of the self-concept of the long-term unemployed and we see you as PhD material." The opposite holds true for those who resent having a white student integrate their black institution. There are times I understand what the professor is looking for and times when it doesn't matter what I turn in.

January 11, 1968

Dear Loretta;

Just finished my last term paper. Eighty-four pages – man, I was sweating blood for a while. I didn't think I was ever going to get it together. It is due Friday at 11:00 AM. It is now 3:00 AM Thursday. Guess I had lots of time anyway.

The test in Statistics went really well. Should have gotten 100. I need it. I have a low B in that course and the professor hates the intrusion of honkeys. I really wanted to get an A in Statistics because you need a good background here for research and research is where the money is in sociology. An example of reverse prejudice: the last test in Statistics I got 2 wrong and a C+ on my paper. Next to me was a guy who got 5 wrong and a B+. Like a damn fool, I asked how come – the answer: "I never take anything away from anybody. Two wrong is a C – if I thought you needed a little help; I gave you additional points. That's my business." Black Power – baby.

I actually stole the term "Black Power" from Stokely Carmichael. He popularized it a couple years ago when he was the head of SNCC.

Sorry to have shaken you up with that 'emergency' call the other night. I must have been feeling 'high' when I read your letter and misinterpreted certain passages. When I talked to you, I realized what I had done. Talk about deflating my ego! In all seriousness, Loretta – I LOVE YOU, NEED YOU AND WANT YOU. JUST YOU! I would marry you tomorrow if I thought that you would be happy with me. It is only my concern for your happiness that makes me realize that maybe

we do need more time to test our relationship. I would rather
lose you than to wake one day and realize that I made you
unhappy – for any reason. When you decide what you want, I
hope I will be the one that can give and share it with you.

If I could be with you right now, I could dress up that proposal
a lot with little hugs and squeezes. I'm daydreaming right now.
It has taken me an hour to write what I have here. Hope I don't
sound punchy! I will make another attempt soon.

Love ya-
Dew

Friday, January 12, 1968

Happy Birthday Good-looking;

I was afraid, what with the pressure of finals that I would forget
your birthday so am a little early. I wish that I could take you
shopping for your present – in a jewelry store maybe – and let
you pick it out yourself but thought this would be second best.
And I wish I could give you more but I am one of the hard-core
poverty people right now. Someday maybe – huh. Loretta, I
have lost track of how much I owe you for the telephone calls
but I would appreciate it if you would pay it up with this check
and take the rest and buy yourself something. I hope there is at
least enough for you and Jane to have a 20-cent beer. And think
of me, just a little, when…

Yesterday, I went and straightened out my union dues. It
cost me $96.00. I almost fainted. The secretary of the union
here charged me on the minimum scale even though I hadn't

worked. This I think is wrong, because the International made a ruling that students were supposed to pay dues on only what they made. We argued it but then he pointed out that I was already on the verge of being delinquent so I paid the amount he wanted with the stipulation that I was going to appeal to the International. Anyway, I have a paid-up working card and now I am going to call Great Falls or Butte and see if there are any steady situations available. So, might be seeing you soon.

As we discussed on the phone, I am seriously planning to drop from the program here. Three others out of the nine are also going to drop. At the last meeting, Wednesday, we made our intentions known. The department head really lost his cools – he got really mad and said we were being unfair to the school and the program. Then he said to do as we pleased, that none of us were capable students anyway, and were anticipated dropouts. The four that plan to drop, including me, had higher grades in all of our classes than anyone in the department, so he had better dream up a better justification than that. But now I am a little worried what this might do to our final grades – but if they mess with me, I will fight them tooth and nail – that they had better believe.

Well, how is everything with my sugar? Have you broken your arm? Not much word from God's country! I had better not gripe because the next couple of weeks will have me tied up. Hope you will understand…I will call you when I'm finished with finals and let you know how I did. In the meantime, I hope you will keep me in good spirits with your cards and letters.

Hey, what did you think when you got that last letter? Bet you thought that I had flipped. Well, that is exactly what I did. I had been studying and kept thinking about us. I sat down and was going to write a long letter explaining exactly how I felt… about waiting and testing our relationship…and then blah. Oh well, I think I did manage to tell you that I love you for what that is worth! When I started to write, I realized that you were right as usual. It made me a little sick inside to realize that I still hadn't won you and it might very well be that you might someday belong to someone else. Then I thought again, that if I wasn't what you wanted and needed, that it would be miserable for you and in turn more miserable for me if we made any hasty decisions that would bind us together forever.

I really do wish that I knew what you wanted. What you want will determine what I will do with my life the next few years. Do you want a professor, a successful business man, a PhD in research or a cowboy (alright I'll scratch the last category)? Really, I am just egotistic enough to believe that what you want, I can get. Somehow though, I wish that what you want and need is someone to just love and care for you. This, I know I could handle…this is what I would like to do for my life's work. OH, OH, I think I'm getting too far out again.

That what will be, will be. Regardless…happy birthday. All my love goes out to you on the big day.

Man, I sure get corny trying to tell you that I think you are the most wonderful thing that ever happened to the world. Wish I could be 'cool' and still get the word across.

Forever yours,
Dew

Hey – now I'm sounding like a candy bar salesman or something! Somedays...

Birthday smooches xoxxooxo and a little whisper of "I love you."

Sunday, January 14, 1968

Dear Loretta;

Just a short note to let you know that "baby, you're on my mind."

I am really proud of myself today. I have been studying since eleven o'clock this morning and it is now eleven o'clock in the evening. I took one break to eat supper. If I had this ambition every day and didn't have to write term papers, I would have straight A's – that is if I were anywhere else but here. I told you that I had received my thesis proposal back from the first reader (a pretty good guy, displays no signs of prejudice) and it was in good shape – well, the second reader tore it apart. Nothing that I can't overcome but it will take redoing and hours of work. I will have to admit that the criticisms were constructive but it changed the entire objective of the thesis. Oh well, no sweat – huh, Sweet Pea? Final exams are staring me in the face – they start this week and carry over until Saturday. They are scheduling seminars which we are obligated to attend during the final week – groan, groan.

Say kid, I must have really shaken you up with the last couple of letters. No word from you! I try and rationalize that with the bad weather around the country that the mail might be tied up someplace. But then again, I must admit that my propositions might have received a negative response and you are searching for a nice way to tell me to cool it. Well, you know me, I want it told like it is. No use playing games.

We are experiencing a cold wave here. It has been sleeting and it even snowed...about ½ inch. You would not believe the reaction of the people. School closed, stores and businesses closed, people were warned not to leave their homes and the freeways were blockaded and closed. You would think they had four feet of snow! The temperature drops down to about 22 degrees above at night and goes up to 35 or 40 degrees during the day. Just right for me.

Well, I have a lot more to say but time and inhibition doesn't permit me to continue. Anyway, you are probably tired of the way I've been carrying on lately. I won't bother to apologize. It is because 'I DO' ...and that's the way it is!

Regards,
Dew

Sunday, January 21, 1968

Hi Scrumptious,

Just taking a break. It is 3:30 AM and am not even beginning to study for a test Monday. I have been studying for a test on Wednesday. It is going to be a bear! We have our notes plus 42 concepts that we have to know at least three definitions for and then the text. Man, right now I don't know which way is up.

I had a test today in Statistics. I think I did okay – but you never know. The test today was on problem working and then we have another test Monday on theory. I thought I'd be weak on calculations but feel 'uptight' on the theory part. I have an 89 average so still a chance for an A.

Hey, excuse the paper. I turned this rat's nest upside down looking for typing paper but am all out. Do you know that I've gone through two boxes of paper? I know that I haven't written you that much so it must have been all term papers -- --oops, forgot about those sordid letters to 'what's her name!'

Man, I know I'm in trouble. I have been writing these sad and depressing letters and complaining about no letters and all – so what happens...today I get three letters from you. I tried to call you twice, but you had a date or something. I was going to call at twelve – your time – but got to studying so hard that now you are probably in bed...dreaming about 'what's his name.'

Your letters really gave me a needed lift today. You little sugar, you...you really write tantalus notes. I almost caught the first flight to Bozeman...good thing I didn't, you were out. But you did make me feel necessary and gave me feelings of aspiration. Every word seems to excite desire...a kind of desire that right now seems unquenchable. I hope that destiny will treat us kindly and that our relationship will grow from one of tantalizing expectation to auspicious fulfillment. (Hey...I don't sound so unaffectionate!) I DO...love you.

Kid, you have really had problems. I wish I were there to help out somehow. But the thing that worries me is your health. Take care and eat right, get lots of rest, and stuff. Really, to me, your health is the most important thing a person can have. All other things are relative.

Yeah, I'm sorry about that cowgirl suit...Sears didn't carry one in size 44. But I will try and make it all up to you some day. In the meantime, I am sending my very own cow-boots to you. Hope they fit. (On second thought, I will just stomp on up there and give them to you in person.)

I was going to send pictures to you with this letter but just checked and they won't fit in the envelope. I will have to pick one up. There are some real dillies.

I hope by now you have cooled off from my previous cold, harsh, and dumb letters. Now, I will try and tell ya how I feel. Great...just great. I realize more every day that you are the beautiful, charming, lovable and MATURE type young lady that I have been in search of for 29 years. Very seriously, ...

I feel very bad when I find out that I have hurt your feelings because of remarks (that I mean to be good-natured kidding) and because at times I act and sound aloof. I hope, that even in our short acquaintance, you realize I am very affectionate and someday have an abundance of love that is waiting to be shared with someone who wants it and will put up with the rest of me.

Man, my mind gets messed up when I start talking that way when you're not here beside me to reassure me.

Well, gotta go...love ya.

Yours in rapturous passion,
Dew

P.S. I still think "regards" is okay.

Wednesday, January 24, 1968

Hi Good-looking!

Just got home from taking a final. I had two today. I think I might have goofed up a bit on this morning's test. But I feel that I did pretty well tonight. I got back my paper in Methods today – that is the one that will lead me to a thesis – I got an 'A'! I felt good about it because it was the only 'A' and he put some complementary remarks inside. In the class this morning, the professor left and said we were on our honor. Huh, some honor. Evidently, the test was out. It really gripes me because I have been studying like a fool...staying up at night. I suppose I could have cheated too but I've never done it and think I would get so nervous that I would probably copy the wrong answer!

I got a cute LITTLE card from you today. Say, where is that job at that you filled your application for. I hope it has a newspaper and better yet a university with a graduate program. The money sounds great – wow—it scares me. What do you need me for?

How come you wrote on the card that you didn't go to the dance but told me on the phone that you did? Just for that I'm gonna take Liza to the movie 'Cool Foot Lukas' (aka 'Cool Hand Luke').

I am pooped and cannot think of what to say. Just two more tests to go. One Friday and the other Saturday. I will rest Saturday and then work at the Journal Sunday night. Preparing to move on!

I think about you a lot, kid. Even having dreams – which is unusual for me…must not be eating right. How did you like the last letter? You didn't know I had it in me, did you? Kid, I love you –and I want to be able to show you affection and not write you about it.

Awful tired. Gotta hit the sack. See ya in my dreams. xoxoxoxoxoxoxxx never too tired to smooch a little. I did, I do, and I will!

With love,
Me

15

Lonely

Weekends, feeling all alone, are the hardest to endure. Loretta is constantly on my mind and I often think of her sweet kisses and soft touch only to be reminded how far away she is. Selfishly, I don't want her to date other guys and find myself very jealous. Quoting a French poet, I tell her: *L'amour sans jalousie, ne peut pas etre l'amour du tout.* If my French is up to par, I think he was saying that: *Love without jealousy cannot be love at all.*

As difficult as it is, I call and tell her, "I don't want you to waste away because you're waiting for me. I want you but I also want you to be happy and satisfied. Much of your beauty radiates from deep within you and it would sadden me forever if I tarnish that beauty."

Loretta responds, "I love you Duane and probably always will but I had hoped by now we would be together to allow our relationship to grow. I find myself questioning it if I don't receive a call or letter from you.

Venturing out the following night to mail Loretta a letter, I come across the "Red Barron," a place with live music. The billboard introduces the singer, unknown to me, as Rod McKuen. I enter the place and listen to him sing *The Sea, the Earth, and the Sky* as I savor my drink, the words reach into my heart and steal my thoughts of Loretta. The song reminds me so much of her that I want to share it. This album is available now on stereo LP so I'll buy it and send it on to her.

Craving people, I decide to go to a movie (at the urging of Bruce and Loretta) and see *Cool Hand Luke*, alone, a first for me. I have never felt so entirely alone. I once again start to question my decision to finish school and be so far away from Loretta.

Pushing myself to study, I write one hundred and two term papers and continue to gather research at the Atlanta Employment Evaluation & Service Center, I move forward somehow. Now accepted by blacks, but rejected by whites, this is a new phenomenon for me. I enjoy getting to know the administrative people Miss White, Mrs. Brown, and Bill at the Center, but find I connect more with Arthur Askew, Clotell, and Troy King.

On Thursday afternoon, Troy approaches me, "Hey man, "What ya got cooking this weekend?"

"Not much, I usually just study," I respond meekly. I silently question myself, *what have I become? I'm living a different lifestyle, for me anyhow. Interacting with few people and making no attempt to develop friendships, I spend my time with my nose in my books twelve hours a day.*

"How about coming with me, my girlfriend Doreen, and Clotell, if she wants to join us, to this local club called Ruby Red's Warehouse?"

"I don't think I have enough money to cover a night out," I hesitate.

"No worries, I have connections with the band manager so no need to worry about money," he offers. "This club opened in January of 1966 and it's a happening place. They have really long lines on the weekend."

"Who is playing tomorrow night? And where is it?" I ask as I might need to make an excuse.

"It's downtown Atlanta at 58 Ellis Street. My friend tells me Aretha Franklin is the main performer."

"So, the only thing is if Clotell wants to be my date?" I excitedly ask. I immediately start to feel guilty about Loretta, only to recall our last phone call and reflect on *her wanting to enjoy her last year in college and have the freedom to date.*

I pick up Clotell in southeast Atlanta, a middle-class neighborhood in a house similar to my parent's house back home. Many of the postwar homes built after World War II seem to duplicate the same style, no matter if they are in the North or South.

We reach the club and the line weaves around the corner of the block. The billboard proclaims *1967—The Year of Aretha Franklin.* Troy appears with his band manager pal and I'm very impressed as his friend takes us past the line motioning for us to follow him to the second row of seats, front and right of center stage. Ruby Red's capacity is stretched to standing room only. Troy turns to me and says, "Aretha is the most popular black woman we have seen. We get down with her when she sings about the things we are feeling like racial tension and Civil Rights."

Ruby Red's Band starts the concert and plays for the first fifteen minutes and then announces Aretha and her *Summer of Soul* music tour. Aretha is dressed in choir attire, probably from her pastor father's church. There is a short huddle between the entertainers when Aretha steps forward and introduces her band members to a modest applause. She is accompanied by her own bass player and the Warehouse provides Ernie Carson as the piano accompaniment. In her hot-buttered voice, she says, "We apologize for the lack of programs but we are going to be starting with my gospel roots and then my new sounds of rhythm and blues melted in." She sings, *I Say a Little Prayer.* Receiving loud applause, she stops to announce, "A woman only wants one thing and that's respect," as she belts out her new hit!

R-E-S-P-E-C-T

Find out what it means to me

R-E-S-P-E-C-T

This is followed by an hour's worth of songs familiar to the South and well-received by the crowd. Aretha then says, "We will take a twenty-minute break so you can get to know each other and consume some beer and roasted peanuts."

A staff of burly waiters yell out, "Ice cold draft beer, roasted peanuts for sale!" as they crunch on the shells under their feet. We stand and decide to go to the concession center although the crowds slow our attempt to leave our row. A mixed group of male and female students in the front row utter quietly, "Wow, did you see that guy in the row behind us. We're just not safe anymore when some coloreds pass as white." His party all turn and their observation seems true.

Troy, Doreen, Clotell, and I make our way to the lobby and Troy offers to buy us a beer and a basket of roasted peanuts. Doreen and Clotell turn down the offer while I ask Troy, "Do you need any help with the bill?"

We return to our seats and Troy follows shortly with two plastic cups of beer, forgetting the peanuts. Aretha is back on stage and nods, saying, "I am so glad to see all of you attend our concert. Do you go to college or where are all of you from?"

Troy responds, "We are from Atlanta and are attending Atlanta University."

"What a fine-looking group! Looks like you have schoolteachers as parents." She looks at me, "I can't guess your Mama's vocation but I am glad to see you here."

The second half of the concert goes for over an hour and includes a number of songs that I enjoy but don't recognize. Looking down at the color of my skin, I almost feel startled to see that I am still white!

Returning to my apartment I immediately check the mail. Finding a letter from Loretta, it seems ironic that she asks if she will *know* me when I return or if I have changed too much. The phenomenon that I'm experiencing has changed my attitude and disposition, which is to be expected. It scares me not knowing how I've changed and what this experience will represent in the long run. Returning to Montana where whites are the majority will definitely be an adjustment.

There have been Civil Rights demonstrations in Atlanta and racial tensions are high throughout the South. There's a lot of literature regarding police brutality, which is passed out on the Atlanta University campus, initiating Black Power discussions that interrupt classes. It is too depressing for me to think much about home.

Friday, February 2, 1968

Dearest Lor,

Just got your card announcing the arrival of Carol Ann and LaVern's little girl. I should get a card and send it to them but you know how swift I am about sending cards. Besides I don't have their address. So please relay the congratulations on to them for me please.

It was great talking to you last night. I felt much better knowing how you felt about my continuing with grad school down here. Once again, you came through and proved yourself an understanding and mature woman...a very rare animal...and as good looking as you are too!

I have piles of work to do again. At the start of every semester it seems as though it will be impossible to wade through the assignments. So far, I have 102 term papers plus weekly

problems in Advanced Statistics. Groan! But someone before
me must have been able to do it and they never had the reason
to be motivated that I have. So, my Advanced Social Statistics
(my weakest subject last semester but a requirement for
persons in the fellowship); Contemporary Sociological Theory
(a required course for all grad students and one I'm sure I will
be able to wade through); Seminar on the Sociology of Poverty
(a unique course which is being taught for the first time this
semester, also required for fellowship but one that shouldn't
prove too difficult); and Advanced Social Psychology (this is
a bear, the prof is the one that piles on the term papers and
treats each one as if it were a PhD dissertation...also required
for fellowship) are my classes. Normally this is a full load but I
am required to take Field Studies and Sociology Seminar, two
blah courses but ones that take up time. Do you think I will
have much time to see Liza? I only hope that I'll have time to
work on my thesis so when June comes around, I can take my
comprehensives and then defend my thesis. And then I will
settle down to the serious business of courting you...if you
haven't run off with some 'slick.'

I am anxiously anticipating March. I hope the weather holds
out and that it doesn't rain. If it does, we'll go down to Daytona
Beach...where it is always warm. But I hope to be able to show
you Atlanta, really a swinging metropolis with everything
imaginable to do. I stopped by the Holiday Inn which is only
about four blocks from my rat's nest and checked on a single
for you and asked about reservations. They said that about
two weeks is good for getting reservations so let me know if you
plan to come alone or if you will bring someone with...okay?

Also, let me know the cost of the plane ticket and flight number so I can send you enough to get down here...I think I will make you get back on your own with the hopes that you won't be able to do it, naturally.

Wow, I'm on the second page and still have lots more to say. Not bad for a guy that can't spell...huh?

I plan to get most of my assignments done that are due next week tonight and then work at the Journal tomorrow night. I need the money for my SWEET PEA. I hope you'll always be my Sweet Pea.

I am sending the pics home that have been promised for a month now. They are not all that great, except the ones with you.

Just caught myself daydreaming about you...you can't imagine how much I miss you or love you. I hope that you will never get tired of being told how beautiful and desirable you are to me!

Guess I shouldn't have bragged about how much more I had to say...all of a sudden, I have become inhibited...about attempting to express myself on paper. I trust that you will find it possible to remember moments when I was less mute and that you find some reassurance from those thoughts.

Be of good cheer now and I will soon set myself in front of this terrifying machine and pay tribute to the one I love.

All my love – forever and a day,
Dew

Sunday, February 4, 1968

My Loved One,

I left my nest to mail your letter last night and to grab a bite to eat. After I dropped the letter, I found this little hideaway – I think it was called the 'Red Barron.' It looked a little rich for my blood but I felt careless and I went in. They had live entertainment – this guy that recorded "The Sea, The Earth, and The Sky" is what the billboard said. I think his name was Rod McKuen. So what?

I had dinner and listened – then I stayed to have a drink. The music and especially the words were or seemed to be exactly what I had tried to say to you so many times and somehow had failed. I come home now with the feeling still a part of me and wanted to sit down and tell you how much I love you – Loretta Nepil. I will not try to steal anything I've heard but somehow, I feel that the composer of the music reached into my heart and stole my thoughts. At one time they sang about parting the sky and reaching for you and I thought of the many times I had tried to do exactly that. They say this outfit is on wax so will buy their album and send it to you. Listen and think of me... for it is me. More than that I somehow imagine it is you and I.

Damned if I'm not high. And I have not drank that much. It is the thought of being with you and maybe a part of you that has sent me on this wild trip. I am on my way to bed...to think and dream of you...being close to me and...and...oh hell and what? I hope I will have enough guts to mail this to you when I wake. It must sound crazy but between the lines is written "I LOVE

YOU" if and I hope you will read...because I do! Here's a big smooch before I go – see you later!

NEXT DAY:

Well today I'm a little bit more sober and inhibited. But just the same I do love you and guess I haven't really said anything that bad. I had you on my mind all night and all day...can't wait to see you. The music I was referring to probably isn't that great but somehow it reminded me of you. I no doubt would have felt the same if I had happened to listen to Marty Robbins. Just the same I am going to buy the album and send it to you.

Missing you very much. Now, I wonder if I made a mistake by staying for the second semester. Hope I haven't pushed my luck. Give my regards to all. Write later.

Faithfully yours,
Dew

Hugs et kisses – xoxoxoxoxo

Thursday, February 8, 1968

Miss Nepil,

I just returned from a night class. It is kinda cold down here tonight. We got a bit of snow last night and for the first time I had to wear a coat to class. It is about 28 degrees right now...I don't know if I can take it.

I know you like the formal intro but had just read your letter describing injuries to your elbow...and when you are in need of a lecture, I like to call you that...it gets your attention. Now, you know you are not any more accident prone than a 1929

Chevy without brakes so don't start developing a complex...
and besides I think you're just trying to discourage me...no
luck, I love you anyway. I don't think I could prevent such
incidents from occurring but agree that it would be good to
be near you...at least I could provide some love and care. On
the serious side, Miss Nepil, I do wish you would be especially
careful the next month or so...I don't want anything happening
to you that would prevent you from coming down. I hope you
are still planning the trip.

Today, I started testing people for my study. I got three. I am
hoping to get about ten a week for a total of 50+. I am really
excited...it is a giant step towards that M.A. As far as I know I
am the only one in my class that has started with the collection
of data and there is only one other student (from Africa) that
has had his research design and thesis proposal approved.
Great, huh?

Other than school I am not doing much. I am really living a
different sort of life than ever before...that is it is different for
me. I have made very few friends and do not attempt to...I
interact with few people and find myself with nose in books
about 12 hours a day. I can't say I enjoy it or even wish to
tolerate it but the desire to obtain the M.A. has seemed to have
caught me up in a current. I hope it gets me to wherever you
will be for the next 50 or so years.

Talking about books, I have a chapter in Statistics to do
tonight plus some problems. I wish there was some way we
could communicate other than by letter. Miss you much, kid,
and appreciate you being you, so never change. Good night
Sweet Pea.

I do...
Me

Sunday, February 11, 1968

Dear Folks,

Not a thing to report on but I thought I had better report in or you would have the law looking for me. I am in good health and fair spirits. I weighted myself at Bruce's house the other day and weighted 158 lbs. So, I am just about right, I think. I have been getting plenty of sleep...in fact too much. Yesterday I went to a movie, just to break the monotony of doing school work. After, I went and had a T-bone and a couple of beers. So, I am living quite affluently.

I have the spring semester 'blahs' ...it seems I have always had a tendency to procrastinate during the spring semester. As usual the work has been piled on and at this stage of the game it almost seems impossible to get it all done. I don't think this semester is going to be as hard as the last. But I might be fooling myself. I have two very difficult courses---Advanced Statistics and Advanced Social Psychology. But I'll give them hell and see what happens.

I guess you've heard of the problems they are having here in the South again. I haven't observed any great increase of bitterness around our campus, so am hoping that they will continue to put up with us honkeys and not decide to take any of their frustrations out on us. It was kinda bad after grades were released and they found out about my A's. Naturally they resent that sort of thing and misplace the cause of grades on the color of one's skin. I lost what rapport I had with most of the students. But I have come to care less what they think of me and am only on campus to attend classes. I use the public library or buy books that I need to do my papers...so have withdrawn from campus life.

How has everyone been? Long time, no hear. I am especially interested to hear how Kim and Kent are doing. I hope Kimmy is finding reading enjoyable. Of course, you know that the basic ability to read is the key to future success in anything. I hope Bonny and Terry continue to show interest in the kids' school work. This means a lot to youngsters. How did Kent make out on his last trip to Rochester? I do wish Bonny could take the time and bring me up to date.

How has Dad been? I hope the license plate buying is just about wrapped up for this year, and that the weather is decent. I hope he gets time to go fishing and to 'mess around' ...that is, I hope that he takes time. Man, in August we are going to go on some kind of excursion. We'll go in the hills someplace and pitch a tent and thumb our noses at the world. I think I'll need that very much by the time this is over. I don't believe I'll be home before then. I have very short breaks between spring and summer semesters. And it is hardly worth the expense to travel all that distance and spend three or four days trying to rest up for the return trip. But you can never tell when the urge to come home surpasses my stinginess. So, don't be too surprised if I just walk in (now don't take this as an attempted hint that I am coming home and start running yourself ragged cleaning and all that other foolishness).

Oh, I just remembered. One reason that I will not be able to come home this summer is because I am working on the collection of data for my thesis. I started this last week to administer the test that will be used as my instrument in testing the causal relationship between variables involved in my study. I am doing a study on the self-concept on the long-term unemployed. Self-concept refers to the attitudes of themselves. I am the only one in my class that is at this stage of the thesis and am one of two students that have had their thesis proposals accepted by the department. So, I am really tickled about that. I just hope I haven't bit off more than I can chew. The study is really original and pertinent to understanding more about poverty. But there is all sort of problems that arise when you attempt to measure attitudes and infer what I'll attempt to infer. Of course, all depends on the outcome of the instrument so can't anticipate too much right now. But wish me luck, because for good or bad, I've jumped in.

How is Adam...and the old homestead? Hope all is going well. What color of Buick does he have now? And how is the union business coming along...he hasn't been drafted by international yet has he? It is really too bad that Adam didn't go full-time union long ago. I am sure that he would have been a damn good executive for the Teamsters.

Well, guess I'll go put the coffee pot on and start in on some reading. Brack...I have some problems to finish in Statistics for tomorrow, too. Groan, groan!

Take care and write when you have a chance. Give my regards to all.

Love and respect,
Son—Duane

My framed Christmas present from Loretta

Double dating for New Year's Eve with Loretta's sister and husband

It feels good to be in my hunting outfit

Studying in my apartment

Loretta's visit in June 1968

Finishing my M.A. Degree

16

Challenges In A Long-Distance Love

When I said goodbye to Loretta in September 1967, I wasn't sure our love would survive over the time and distance. Many obstacles would have to be conquered. Her intuition told her one week after meeting me that we would marry one day.

I was concerned, but kept it to myself, that if I didn't make it home for Christmas our fragile relationship could splinter. After spending a few days with her over Christmas vacation, I am deeply in love and want to be engaged and marry soon. She cautions me that, "We have an eight and one-half-year difference in our age and I'm Catholic and you're Lutheran." She fails to mention that my brief first marriage could take years to annul and may need intervention from His Holiness, the Pope.

Due to the high costs of telephone calls, our love letters serve as our source of communication. Misunderstandings easily crop up and soon fester. I begin chasing her in earnest in January although she doesn't want to commit yet and remains cool as a cucumber. I am shaken that she wants to be free to date in her final year of college. We make plans for her to visit me during our respective spring breaks. Our plans are shattered, however, when we learn that a printing mistake in Atlanta University's vacation schedule means that our mutual spring breaks will not align. Feeling guilty, I profess, "Loretta, I'm not sure our love for each other will endure until we see each other again."

My assignments, term papers, and the data gathering for my thesis pile up, leaving little time to write letters. I struggle with the sacrifice of committing to the graduate program, with all of its racial tensions, and my love for her. I admit that I have held her too long, and release her. Loretta is strong, and very mature for a barely twenty-one-year-old woman. After receiving three wonderful letters in a week's time, I realize I have misunderstood her true feelings.

Saturday, February 3, 1968

Dear Loretta,

Just a short note to let you know how lonesome I am for you. I really have the blahs today. I did not work tonight because I went golfing with Bruce Stone and did not get back in time. Brack – as you would say.

I want to call you so very much tonight but swore I would cut down on calling so I would have the extra change to show you a good time when you get here. I sure hope nothing comes up to interfere with our plans.

Any more news concerning where you might be next fall? Let me know as soon as you make a decision so I can inquire about work. No sweat, though, because I am hoping that we can sit down together when you are here and make some tentative plans.

I hope you keep the good work up in school. I am really proud of you. I am always proud of you no matter what it concerns. I am the one that had better try and hold on to you...you know you've hooked me.

Well another weekend has gone by without you. I think the weekends are the hardest to take. During the week I always seem busy with school but on the week-ends I seem to have you on my mind constantly. It is good to think of you and remember the wetness of your kisses and the softness of your touch but it is saddening to realize how far away you are from me. It is selfish of me to want you to not take part in campus life and date other guys but if I were not jealous of you, I would question my sincerity when I say...I love you. A French poet once said "L'amour sans la jalousie, n'est pas l'amour aucunment." I think, if my understanding of French is correct, he was saying that love without jealousy cannot be love at all!

I have got to get busy on assignments due Monday. I will write again tomorrow and hope that I will be in a cheerful mood. Sorry for the blah letter...will make up it someway – someday. Regardless of the mood I'm in, I love you. It is moods like this that make me realize how much I need you...I need to hold you, to touch you and be able to whisper dumb little things in your ear and to punctuate them with soft nibbles. Tomorrow seems a century off and March is lost in infinity.

Can you tell – I STILL DO?

Faithfully yours,
Dew

P.S. don't be so stingy with the smooches!
xoxxooxo(breathe) xoxo I love you.

Wednesday, February 7, 1968

Dearest Loretta,

I received two letters from you yesterday. One really cheered me up and the other made me wish, I had died. But I love and respect you for telling me how you feel. Loretta, I cannot help feel guilty for the way you feel. I want you to enjoy your last year in college and if you will enjoy it more by dating, please date. I trust you more than my own mother and know you are above reproach. If it happens that you meet someone you love more than me then I could only wish both of you the very best. If you want me home to be able to date you then, sweetheart, I'm on my way. But all I ask is for you to be happy...enjoy being young and beautiful!!!

The European tour sounds great. We will have to discuss it when we see each other. Maybe I could pose as your husband and could go with...it would make an ideal honeymoon...huh? Again, I feel guilty...it seems that I am tying you down too soon in your young life. I know the value, especially for personal development, that travel has. I would not trade my travels for a million dollars unless I could use the million for more travel. It would be beyond my wildest dream to have shared the miles I have travelled with you. But I do dream about the day when we might be 'fellow travelers' ...oops, getting misty thinking about just being with you.

Hey, I dug the article about CGF. Sounds like a stunt Teddy would pull. It must be tough to lose a loved one.

I am waiting anxiously for more word about your plans in March. I am determined to have all my work done before then and to be in good shape for a carefree time. I am behind right now but will put it in high gear and motate.

In parting, I want to again remind you to not waste away because of me. I love you too much – to ever want that. I want you, but I want the happy and satisfied Loretta that I once knew. Although you are fortunate to possess much physical beauty, much of the beauty I saw in you radiated from deep within you and it would sadden me forever if I thought I had tarnished even a bit of that beauty. So...be beautiful...I'll love you forever.

Just me –
Dew

Sunday, February 11, 1968

Dearest Loretta,

I am happy to hear that nothing serious was involved in the injury to your arm and that it is on its way to recovery. Be careful, sweetie!

Yesterday, I finally found that album, 'The Sea'. I bought it and sent it to you. I hope you have it by now. I really can't remember what it was like but when I heard the music it reminded me of you so much that I wanted to share it with you. I hope the recording does justice to the real thing. (I had it gift wrapped and then forgot to even enclose a card – dumb, dumb.)

Last night I finally got to see the movie 'Cool Hand Luke'... man what a loser. I hope I'm not like that...it scares me though because you and Bruce Stone both said that Luke reminded you a little of me – ouch. Cool it baby, you know I don't look good in stripes. I went to the movie alone. It was the first time, that I can remember, that I went to a movie alone. It was a strange experience...but one that I have grown used to lately. I have never been so entirely alone before in my life. I have always had someone to buddy around with...even in Havre, I had Frank Hayes and you. It is different to observe and feel things and then have to internalize them because of the lack of someone to communicate with. Sometime, we'll have to sit down and talk about all my strange experiences...ok?

Well, again, time is pressing. I have three problems to do for Statistics tomorrow. I just wanted to remind you that I still care very much for you and am anxiously waiting for the time when we may be together once again. Remember that you are beautiful...and keep smiling. I love you.
Duane

Sunday, February 18, 1968

Dear Loretta,

About that phone call...I am not sure it was you I talked to at all. The person I talked to did not resemble the Loretta I know...or knew! Your letters have not given me a hint of anything wrong...is there something bothering you, kid? It isn't like you to keep something like that from me...is it someone else? I hope I get a letter soon that will ease my mind.

I am really bogged down with work. I am still having problems with Statistics...I don't know why I signed up for the advanced course. We are working problems that use trigonometry and calculus and I have no background in math, whatsoever. So, I am in the process of teaching myself how to add and subtract and still trying to keep up with daily assignments. And I thought this semester was going to be easier.

Sweetheart, I am going to call tonight. I am so bothered over that last call. Can't seem to communicate...forgive me for the shorty. I love you and need you more than ever.

I will try again when I'm in a better mood. Have I made a mistake by loving you as much as I do? I do, you know, so much it hurts.

Forever and ever,
Dew

Sunday, February 26, 1968

Dear Loretta,

I have just tried to call you and again, you were not in. I am a little upset because I was told to call at 9 o'clock your time and this I did and still – no Loretta. The last couple of weeks I have tried to call several times with the same results...so it looks like you are keeping yourself pretty busy outside the dorm.

I have been going day and night in an effort to get my assignments caught up so I would be free during March. I realize that my letter-writing has suffered because of this. But I did not expect you to respond in the manner which you did. Statements like: Get on the ball or else forget it...sort have made me believe that you do not realize or appreciate what I am doing or why I was doing it. Grad school is not a fraternity picnic.

Loretta, I have always realized that many obstacles would have to be overcome if I was going to be fortunate to marry you. I had faith that these obstacles could be subdued but realized that you would have to be patient and considerate. I sincerely question that fact at this time if you care enough for me and if you could be patient enough or considerate enough to want to wait for me. I am the first one to admit that you would probably be a fool to do so but some-how I had seen all these attributes in you that led me to believe and to have faith that someday soon we would be able to share a happy and fulfilling life. Now, I don't know. It seems that everything has to go your way or else...forget it!

Again, I am faced with the demands of school and the demands of a beautiful girl that I love very much. I cannot see how I can do both. I also realize that you would lose confidence in me if I were to fail in school so I am forced to stay with the grad program. I will not ask you to wait any longer...it has been too long already. What I have tried to say is that I cannot afford the time for both you and school. And rather than have you tell me to go to hell...or forget it...I have held you too long and now must admit that I do not deserve you and must release you at last. So...you are free little girl, run away fast.
Duane

Monday, March 4, 1968

Dear Loretta,

I am almost ashamed to sit down and write. It has been too long since I have taken time out and told the one I love how much I do miss her and how I wish I could be with her. On top of everything I received three wonderful letters from you today that made me feel very small. I am fortunate that you are strong and can take into consideration all the faults I have.

What is really hurting me now is the thought I have failed you. I think of you often and it is the thought of being with you that keeps me going. Don't ask me how I can get so wrapped up in school that I won't even bother to take time to write or call you. Sometimes I am on the verge of sitting down and writing and then I just get caught up in the process of reading that next chapter or doing one more problem and then I wake up and it's time to go to class. I just hope that someday I will have the opportunity to make up for it and that you won't be bitter. Loretta, I still love you and need you very much...remember that regardless of what happens.

Loretta, thank you very much for sticking by me in this crisis. I know I must be a retard or have brain damage for being such a damn fool and letting things like last week happen to us. I just hope that it is not too late to make you realize how very much I do care for you. It seems futile to attempt to relate my feelings by way of the U.S. mail but will do it if nothing else is available. I will improve my habits but cannot improve my feelings for you...they are still at a peak that denies measurement. I LOVE YOU. I LOVE YOU. I LOVE YOU.

Yours for infinity,
Duane

Thursday, March 7, 1968

Dear Loretta,

Hi kid. How goes the battle? Just finished reading some theory and am not tired enough to hit the sack, (it's one o'clock) and anticipate a big weekend, so will try to catch up on my writing. I hope to knock out another term paper this weekend and do some studying for Advanced Psychology. We have a test coming up next weekend so I want to be prepared. School is coming along...not as great as I would like, but can't complain.

I just found out that spring break this year doesn't start until the 21st. Someone was asking about mid-terms and we were told that there had been a mistake in the catalog concerning the scheduling of spring break and mid-terms. So, %$#@ ... (that means I was really off base.)

The weather is warming up fast. It is almost uncomfortable wearing a coat and tie. But is cools off at night and one can sleep quite comfortably. I hope I get a chance to get out in the sun and get tanned...but that is probably hopeful wishing... unless I could find a place that is quiet and I could take a book along and study. I am in a rare mood tonight...really 'hung-up' on sociology! At times I really get enthusiastic about research and its importance and all and then (mostly) I just go along wondering what is the use of all the time and effort put into trying to understand man.

I felt a pang of spring fever today...it made me remember last summer...Havre, a certain picnic, a supper and a drive...and I started to get very homesick. I had to repress the feeling and the thought...I can't afford the luxury of thinking a lot about things like that. I'm afraid I am not a very stable person...first thing you know I would be heading west, leaving behind what seven months ago I thought was so important. Sometimes, I wish I didn't have such great control of myself. I wonder what I have grown to be! Strange, the things I find myself doing and not doing.

I hope finals have gone A-Okay for you Sweet Pea. I am sure they did, though. You are a pretty smart young lady...I really believe that.

Cannot get my mind off you and Montana right now. I wish I could be with you to share the coming of spring there. I miss the change of seasons very much. Montana seemed so fresh and young in the spring. Somehow, I equate spring in Montana with you...there is something very promising about you...

Be good to yourself sweetheart. You are a very rare animal. I only wish I could have and hold you forever.

I do,
Duane

Saturday, March 23, 1968

Dear Loretta,

Don't faint, I'm finally getting around to writing. I have had quite a time for the last couple of weeks. I just wish I could have had you to lean on – I needed you badly.

Two weeks ago, I was over at Bruce's. It was a Friday night and we were watching some TV. I had just said to him to remind me to give Bozeman a call at midnight. All of a sudden there were these shots. He jumped up and ran out. I was a little slower getting up and out and when I caught up to him, he was leaning over this guy that had been shot. He had caught a .38 slug two inches under the heart. Man, he was a mess. We put a compress on the wound and called the cops. The guy who had done the shooting had taken off. I stayed with the (what I thought would be a dead man) wounded man while Bruce and his next-door neighbor went looking for the gunman. (Bruce had a shotgun – really didn't show me much. I thought they were damn fools for wanting to get involved.) The cops came and found the guy and finally sent for an ambulance. We found out later the guy lived. The shooting resulted from an argument over a bottle of booze. Right civilized people live here in Georgia. When it was all over, it was three in the morning and needless to say I didn't call you.

I was in a gloomy mood all the next week and if it hadn't been for a couple of wonderful letters from you, I think I would have cracked. I was really being pressured in a couple of courses and it seemed like nothing was going right. I still had guilt feelings about not being able to see you at spring break. I know

it was my fault...but had to make the choice of either a couple of days with you or getting my "bag" together for midterms.
We are on break right now. It is kinda good you didn't come down. We have had tornado warnings out the last couple of days and it has been raining and blowing something fierce. I have taken advantage of the bad weather and have caught up with my term papers. I only have two more to do for the whole semester. That makes me feel good. I am going to study statistics today and tomorrow. That is our first test when we get back – Wednesday. I think I will work at the Journal tomorrow night. I could use the money and it will do me good to have a change of pace.

I learned this last week that my uncle died. He was operated on for cancer and never came out of the operation. He did not know he had cancer and had been sick about ten days. It is sad to lose him but I am glad he never had to suffer long. It really shook my mother and dad – they were very close.

Hey, thanks for the pics of the newborn baby and all. Tell LaVern and Carol Ann that I am jealous. They make a nice-looking family. Sure, wish we could all get together for an evening and spin yarns...and listen to some good 'cow' music.

Loretta, I wish I could tell if you are serious about taking advantage of leap-year. I think you're just teasing though! You had better be careful because I might hold you to your offer. Better yet, when (and I hope it isn't too late) we see each other again I have an offer of my own to negotiate with you. (I say some pretty stupid things, don't I?) How can you negotiate love? Oh well, that's me. I still do love you – very much. I pray that time has not taken its toll and that time is all that we have lost.

I bet I get a "mad letter" from you before you get this, so will try and reach you by phone tonight.

Also, enclosing a check for the telephone bill.

All my love forever,
Duane

17

Tensions Mounting

The night of February 8, 1968, a civil rights protest on the South Carolina State University campus turns deadly. I have heard it is one of the most violent episodes of the civil rights movement, yet it receives very little recognition or press coverage. Students at Spelman College and Atlanta University are trying to raise bail money for the jailed students and SNCC Field Secretary Cleveland Sellers. I receive their literature and mail it to Loretta.

Currently, the Poor People's Campaign, also known as the Poor People's March on Washington, is being organized by Dr. King and the Southern Christian Leadership Conference (SCLC). They believe the civil rights movement didn't improve the material conditions of life for many blacks. "The focus now is that all people should have what they need to live. We will demand economic and human rights for poor Americans of diverse backgrounds. After my visit to the poorest county in the U.S., I want to start the march in Marks, Mississippi, located in Quitman County, and march to Washington," King states. He goes on, "I am announcing a shift in the second phase of the civil rights movement from 'reform' to 'revolution.'" There is some concern that King is getting more radical. Stokely Carmichael preaches the use of violence as a legitimate means of self-defense. I am startled by this new tactic, and wonder what this experience will represent.

There is a rising tension after the released report on February 29, 1968, by the Kerner Commission, who examined the causes of race riots of previous years. They declare "the nation is moving toward two societies, one black, one white—separate but equal." The blacks at Atlanta University say this is a step backward, not forward, after the passage of the Civil Rights Act of 1964 outlawing segregation in public places. Many whites in the South refuse to recognize this.

Martin Luther King, Jr., is now directing his attention to the Memphis Sanitation Strike. On March 28, 1968, he leads a march that turns violent. After King himself is led from the scene, a sixteen-year-old black boy is killed, sixty people are injured, and 150 people are arrested.

Monday, February 12, 1968

Dear Loretta,

We have been having some demonstrations and feelings are quite high all over the south. I read in the newspaper a brief article where highway patrolmen opened fire on 200 unarmed black student protestors at South Carolina State University (SC State). They referred to it as the Orangeburg Massacre. I am enclosing a piece of literature that was passed out on the Atlanta University campus regarding the killing of four and the wounding of 50 in this massacre. Conditions are worsening although cold weather has probably kept anything serious from breaking out. Thursday night we had a class cancelled – I guess I told you about that on the phone.

BLACK STUDENTS MURDERED

BLACK PEOPLE THIS CONCERNS US!!!

FOUR BLACK STUDENTS KILLED IN ORANGEBURG, S.C.

50 SHOT!!!

THURSDAY NIGHT, February 8, the police agents of South Carolina (National Guard, State Troopers) opened fire on a group of unarmed students on South Carolina State College campus killing four and wounding 50.

Although the South Carolina National Guard and white authorities have complete control of their local press and have tried to blame the students for provoking the attack, national TV newsmen have verified that the students were UNARMED and no shots came from the students. South Carolina newsmen and National Guard have also tried to lay blame on SNCC Field Secretary Cleveland Sellers, who was shot and injured along with the students. Sellers lives across the street from the college campus, is from nearby Denmark, S.C. and is presently in jail with some 20 other students.

BOND ON SELLERS IS SET AT $50,000. Some reports claim that adequate medical attention has been denied to all those injured.

WHAT BLACK BROTHERS AND SISTERS MUST DO NOW!!!

Money is DESPERATELY NEEDED FOR BOND ON SELLERS AND STUDENTS WHOSE LIVES ARE IN DANGER IN ORANGEGBURG JAIL. All money raised will be used to bond Sellers and those students unable to raise their own bond. CONTACT YOUR FRIENDS AND LOCAL GROUPS, COLLECT MONEY AND SEND IT AT ONCE TO:

ORANGEBURG STUDENT DEFENSE FUND
% Mary Cammack

Spellman (sic) College

Box 226 or Call 404-794-4119

The question we sometimes ask ourselves is not how this
MAN CAN SHOOT US DOWN BUT HOW WE CAN STAND BACK AND LET
HIM GET AWAY WITH IT!!!???

Tuesday, March 5, 1968

Dear Folks,

*Howdy! Just a line of thanks for sending the tape recorder
down. It got here in splendid shape. I was amazed at the
packing job Dad had done. The "Ole Pro" sure knows his stuff.
I am enjoying one of my tapes now while I take this break and
write this letter.*

*I've been taking in some of the lectures at Emory University
and going to the theatre, also getting around to some of the
different Jazz groups in town. I met this psychologist with the
school system here who I met through a PhD friend of mine
from Emory. She is just short of her PhD and is not really
my type but she kinda has adopted me and wants to get me
cultured. Also, she is pretty understanding about my school
work and being short of money and all. She has a pretty
swanky apartment and has me up for Sunday dinner...and she
really puts on a feed. It is very relaxing for me and is almost as
good as a trip home. Nothing serious will develop...I've got too
many other things on my mind to do first.*

*It has started to warm up down here. Today, I felt a little warm
in my coat and tie. But it cools off at night and I sleep well. But*

I can imagine how it will be in a couple of months. They are predicting a long hot summer for Atlanta. I haven't decided if they are referring to the weather or the racial climate... You can feel a mounting tension and very little seems to be being done to avert it (riots).

Dad, I think I will hold off on buying that smaller tape recorder. Bruce has one and we are getting by pretty well. Thanks for the trouble though.

I hope everyone is in good shape, especially the kids. How are they anyway? No word from Bonny. Guess I should take the initiative and write her but I always figured these letters home were common property. Tell her I think about her and Terry and the kids often. I sure hope things go good for those kids... they have worked pretty damn hard and deserve a break. The same goes for you folks too.

Not much of a letter is it? Well, I am thinking of a hundred things I have to get done. I will try to do better this weekend. Say hello to all and take care of your health... Oh, yeah, say hello to Ed Mars for me and tell Mrs. McGee if she wants to be a good sociologist, she should come down here and give the ghetto a whirl for real. Second-hand information and opinions are usually biased and that isn't being scientific, is it? I would like to see some of those do-gooders from the college there have to live in the ghetto a week. The applications for the convent would triple.

Love,
Your son, Duane

Friday, March 8, 1968

Dear Loretta,

I just got home from class. We were kept 30 minutes over. Stokely Carmichael is in Atlanta and a big "black power" discussion developed and we were made to suffer through it. It sounds like even King has announced a shift from "reform" to "revolution" in this 2nd phase of the civil rights movement.

I feel like I'm coming along with assigned term papers on schedule. I have five left to do...two of them are going to be bears. But I am not really sweating them. I thought I was coming along in Statistics until today. We had four problems which took about 2 ½ hours each to do. When I got to class, I found out that I had done every one wrong. I have to do them over...plus a new assignment. We meet three times a week and each time we have six to eight hours problem working to do... plus reading. Stat. is my big hang-up this semester. I think (I know) that it is because of my poor math background. I never had any trigonometry or calculus and it is hurting me now.

I keep questioning why I signed up for Advanced Statistics but it is getting me no where so just need to keep up with the daily assignments and hope that I am doing the problems correctly.

Loretta, I am so thankful that I have you in my life. I would never have made it here without you. I just hope I can hang on to you forever if we are so fortunate to be together. I love you!
Duane

Sunday, March 10, 1968

Dear Folks,

Please excuse the fancy paper. I have been working on term papers and this is all I have available right now. I'm really just disorganized. The place is really a mess. I have books and papers strewn around the apartment...looks like a tornado just passed through.

The weather here has warmed up considerably in the last couple of days. It rained quite hard last night and then cleared today. As a result, it is sort of sultry. But I can't complain, yet. The streams are swollen and very muddy down here. They say they get that way after every rain. I wonder how it affects the fishing? I hope to get a chance to do a little fishing while I'm down here. But will have to wait until this semester is over at least. I'm gonna have to get in gear.

There is not much news that would be of interest to any of you. Dr. Leary was in town preaching drug addiction as an ideal way of life. He was a sad sight...all dressed in East Indian type robes, hair hanging, and generally looking a mess. My opinion is that this man's mind has snapped. I suppose he took one trip too many. Stokely Carmichael is here in Atlanta, holding meetings with black power leaders, and planning for summer activities! It will be interesting to see what they have planned. Nothing is expected to develop until the middle of June or so.

I am enjoying good health and find myself holding up quite well under the 'stresses' of graduate school. Actually, I have found out that regardless of how hard you work you get what the particular professor wants to give you. As a result, I just do

what is necessary to get by and let the cookie crumble as it may.
It might sound like a bad attitude but my hair has stopped
turning grey and I am enjoying life a lot more.

My license cost $43.00 here. Quite a savings over Montana.
People here complain about the car tax but they have no idea
how it is in other places. Also, they have highways and freeways
that Montana will not see for another fifty years. But people
have to complain about something.

I sure would appreciate a note letting me in on the scoop. I
know that it probably seems like nothing exciting is happening
in your lives either but just the same, I am anxious to here
from y'all.

Love and concern,
Son, Duane

Tuesday, March 26, 1968

Dear Folks,

Hi, how is everything? Just finished eating and am going
to settle down to some serious reading. It is really nice here
now—makes it hard to be cooped up in school all day and
then studying all night. But the time is flying and it will soon
be over. Today is the last day of spring break. I spent most of
the break working on my thesis. I have to defend it Thursday
before the faculty and student body—it will be a big sweat but
I will be glad to get over that benchmark. I am the first one
in our class to present my proposal so really don't know what
to expect.

I was shocked and deeply saddened to hear of Uncle Ells's untimely passing. It is times like this that I am bothered not being closer to our families. I want to write Bea, Terry and Gail and...and I don't know who else. I just don't know what to say. God, Terry will be lost. He and his dad were very close from what I observed. More like brothers...if brothers can be closer than father and son? Mom and Dad, I think I'll just buy a sympathy card and not write much. If Mom hasn't already left, please tell her to explain that I just can't express how bad I feel...guess I'm kinda funny that way. I feel that letters are cold and aloof.

I do hope that all else is going well. Please take care of your health and don't overdo the working. I hope the kids are doing well. It sure would be nice to hear from Bonny...but can't blame her for not writing when I never do. Let her know I think of her and the kids often.

I got a haircut on Thursday and had it cut pretty short. Everyone was shocked when they saw me. Guess I had let my hair get pretty long. It was the first trim I have had since Christmas. Then I was told that I had better let it grow out...I looked like a true soul brother with it long. I was also advised to grow a beard. I guess this will be a passport this summer during the anticipated strife. Tension is already mounting. Everyone is concerned. A lot will depend on the weather. If it gets hot early, before most of the college group can get out of school and on summer jobs there is no doubt that there will be trouble. I am not really worried about my own safety. I have gotten along well with most of the radicals and the faculty seems to get wind of trouble brewing and warns us ahead of time. It was some time last week, and they were having a 'black power' meeting on campus. Bruce and I were told to stay away just in case. We stayed away!

Well folks, it's time to get back to the grind. Take care and let me know how everyone is. Please rest assured that I am fine and am in good health.

Your Son,
Duane

Friday, March 30, 1968

Dear Loretta,

Well another month has rolled around and the time is drawing near to the end of this mess down here. No one will be happier than me when it's over. I hardly allow myself to think of home much. It is depressing and I'm already down as far as I can afford to go right now.

You mentioned that you feared that I might have changed too much and that you would not know me when I returned. You must have been receiving mental telepathy waves or something. This very thought has been bothering me very much lately. I know I have experienced phenomenon that has changed my attitudes and disposition – this is natural and to be expected. What scares me is that I really do not know in what direction I have been changed and what exactly the product of this experience represents. I am sure that I will have to readjust to the idea of living in a white majority when I return to Montana. I cannot help but wonder what, if any, the lasting effects will be. I wonder at times where I'm bound, and why. It is hard for me to imagine sharing our lives the way we had talked about so many times...Man, I need to have one of those talks with you right now! Can you tell?

Not much news. We had a test in Statistics today. It took 2 ½ hours. I really felt drained. I think I did pretty well, but I studied hours for it. In fact, I am worried about studying for the final. My mid-term test schedule worked out really great. I have lots of time between tests...this won't be the case with finals. Usually at the finals, we end up with two tests on the same day, and kid, that can be a bear...when they take two to three hours to take.

I am spending the weekend studying...something different? Next couple of weeks will be busy ones. We are having two seminars and I have to speak at both. I have to do research to prepare and then I'll spend a lot more time worrying about the presentation. I want to be sharp because the department head will be there and I want to make a good impression. It will make a difference how you are treated when oral comprehensives come.

Loretta, I really haven't said much. I wish I could write the kind of letters you do. They always seem witty and cheerful and have very positive effects on my morale. I doubt if mine have the same effect for you. But I'll keep plugging away and hope that you will have the time and energy to rehabilitate the old man when he gets back home. We will have to ride to Havre and have dinner at our place out on the highway. That place did the trick once, maybe it will work again. If not, we can

*always stop in at the bowling alley in Fort Benton and hope for
another blackout... remember?*

I love you! I need you!
Duane

18

A Shot Rings Out: April 4, 1968

Another month has rolled around and the time is drawing near to the end of my experience down here. I don't allow myself to think of home for fear of sinking further into depression. Grabbing my rain coat, I step out into pouring rain for my Thursday night class in Research Methods. During class, Dr. Williams receives a note and tells the class the shocking news. He is clearly shaken as he reads:

```
Martin Luther King was killed as he stepped out onto
the balcony of the Lorraine Motel in Memphis, Tennessee
tonight. A lone assassin fatally shot him just after
8:00 p.m. EST.
```

One of the students turns on his radio and we start our break ten minutes later. The radio broadcaster interrupts the programming at 8:15 p.m. EST with the voice of President Johnson coming on the air, "*America is shocked and saddened by the brutal slaying tonight of Dr. Martin Luther King,*" he says.

There is an immediate outpouring of grief and anger. Black Power students are giving Bruce and me hate stares and start approaching us aggressively. I try to anticipate what might happen next. One of the students pulls out a knife and steps toward us seeking revenge. I am horrified when he says, "They got one of ours, let's get one of theirs."

Dr. Williams rushes out and commands, "Class is dismissed, go home *now!*"

Robbie Burns, who at six-foot five inches calls himself a Super Negro yells, "You are not going to do anything to this honky." He picks up my five-foot ten-inch body and carries me over his shoulder gruffly saying, "Don't come back honky until we tell you that it's safe." Bruce who comes in at six feet, is grabbed by the arm by another student and we are escorted out among catcalls and hate stares.

Bruce and I head to his house where we watch the TV coverage in horror. Riots erupted almost immediately throughout the country. In Washington, DC:

> King's death is announced by television and radio at 8:19
> p.m. and by 9:25 p.m. rioters shatter the first store front
> window with a Molotov cocktail. By midnight, buildings
> are engulfed in flames. The fire department logs at least a
> hundred blazes.

Riots break out in more than one hundred cities as the shocking news travels.

On Friday morning, hearing further updates, Bruce calls and tells me, "Students at Atlanta University are planning to march in protests. Mayor Ivan Allen is trying to avoid violence at all costs. He and Geno Patterson, the editor of the *Atlanta Constitution* went on campus earlier and met with the college president where they indicated: *We are aware of the planned march and would like to join the students.*

The students, calling themselves the Black Action Committee, put out a statement declaring *violent retaliation is out.* They reject Allen's offer to march with them. Six college presidents decide to join the march of a thousand participants as it makes its way through Vine City, to 234 Sunset Avenue where King called home at the time of his death.

Bruce explains, "The school has no idea when us honkies can safely return to school."

With the announcement on Thursday night 60 percent of Atlanta residents learn of King's assassination. By 8:00 a.m. the next morning 97 percent of the city knows.

Police are placed on two twelve-hour shifts each day; firemen alter their schedules, and Mayor Allen requests Atlanta University students be used as marshals. I'm concerned for my safety, worried about people taking advantage and using the situation to cause trouble. With people wanting to show their strength or power, I have no idea what will happen.

The local radio station reports very little violence in Atlanta but focuses solely on what we are experiencing as a nation:

Violence escalates in Boston, Winston-Salem, Chicago, New York and Minneapolis. Nineteen hundred federal troops march into Baltimore to quell arson. In Detroit two police officers are shot. Some 57,500 National Guard troops are dispatched to more than 100 cities having riots and fires. On April 7th, Palm Sunday, East Point, a suburban city located southwest of Atlanta is burning.

In Atlanta, tensions are running high with concerns that we will see similar retaliatory violence and fires. It appears to me that the mayor and activists want to foreshadow a sense of peace and calm for the Civil Rights leaders and dignitaries that are planning to attend Dr. King's funeral. Trying to stay abreast of the news, I venture out in the daylight hours to buy a newspaper. Feeling thankful that I no longer live at Ware Hall, I refuse to return to class until I hear from my advisor.

At the West Hunter Street Baptist Church, Pastor Ralph Abernathy presents his sermon as a 'letter' to King. Speaking of the rioters in other cities, he says, *"I want you to know, Martin, we are going to point the way for them."* King's nonviolent vision is preserved in Atlanta.

Governor Lester Maddox refuses to lower the flag at the State Capitol in honor of King, until he is finally told it is a federal mandate.

After days of rain and storms, King's funeral at Ebenezer Baptist Church on April 9th, is a clear and sunny eighty-degree day. His green wooden coffin is placed on a mule-drawn wagon for the four-mile procession to Morehead College, his alma mater. An estimated hundred thousand people quietly wind along the route, where only the echo of mule hooves on the street can be heard. King's tombstone at South View Cemetery is inscribed, "Free at Last! Free at Last! Thank God Almighty, Free at Last!"

Governor Maddox refuses to close the state government or to attend the funeral. He barricades himself inside the State Capitol and stations sixty-four riot-helmeted state troopers at the entrances to protect *the property of the state.* It is reported that he orders troopers to *"Shoot them down and stack them up"* if protestors try to enter the building. Maddox felt King was an *"Enemy of the country."*

Thursday, April 4, 1968

Dear Loretta,

I just got home from Bruce's where we have been watching TV accounts of the assassination of Martin Luther King. Word of the shooting reached us while we were in class. There was quite a commotion when we were outside of the classroom on break. Some of the 'black power' students wanted to go for revenge immediately. One classmate pulled a knife and yelled, "They got one of ours, let's get one of theirs." Class was dismissed and Robbie Burns (who at 6'5" towered over us) along with a couple other Negro students escorted Bruce and myself to our cars. Robbie said, "Don't come back, honkey until we tell you it's safe." We had to go by the library and as we did several cat calls were directed at us. I cannot blame most of the students for being a little emotional at a time like this. I guess I would be too.

We will not attempt to go in until they call us. I hope things have cooled down by Monday. It would be just my luck to have things explode right now when I am ¾ of the way through. But no use being a prophet of doom yet. It is a little early to tell what will be the extent to the reaction.

I tried to call you and my folks but the telephone company was completely snowed under. Atlanta was King's home and headquarters and I suppose civil rights leaders all over the nation have been forwarding their regrets to the family and to King's assistants – I suppose they all are wondering... what's next?

Everything else is going along pretty well. I have been busy but not really bogged down. You will have to excuse the content of this letter. I am a little shaken and am at a loss for words. I will write this weekend and hopefully be in a better mood.

It is pouring rain tonight. We had tornado warnings all afternoon but Atlanta was missed. But, kid, you should just see it rain. It is really coming down in buckets. I wish I had you close to me to keep me warm...and to reassure me tonight. If I ever get home, you can bet that I won't ever stray again.

That's it for tonight. Be beautiful.

Love,
Duane

Tuesday, April 9, 1968

Dear Loretta,

Hi Good-looking! How goes the battle? I suppose you are busy preparing for upcoming tests. Good luck…and remember… keep the faith!

It was good to talk to you last night. I'm sorry if I upset you with my loose talk. I have made up my mind that I will not be shaken or upset by what is going on around me. So, I go about in my own little world, which I have colored a bright pink, and pretty much unaffected by those who are bitter, sad, or scared. I know you could not understand this by our conversation. Sorry!

I don't know when school will resume for us honkeys. I am interested to see what will happen if we miss more than a week of school. I suppose it will be our duty to catch up. It has been a little difficult to study or even read with things the way they are. Not much news is being released to the radio stations because they don't want a panic. I heard that they have had dozens of fires and rock-throwing incidents in Atlanta but nothing real serious. We had a store burn down last night around 12:30 AM about two blocks from where I live. But I don't know if it was set or what. All the stores have been closed today along with gas stations and most restaurants. Things seem quiet here.

It is a lot worse in other places, the newspaper said that nationwide 39 people died, with more than 2,600 injured.

Well, sweetheart, hope you are not upset. I feel relatively safe. I will not take any chances and will not go to school until my advisor says it's okay. If I could, I would fly home for a week or so but I just cannot afford it. I think my folks are in Canada. I have tried to call them but have not been able to get through. I know that they are concerned.

It is getting dark and I don't want to turn on any lights tonight. This neighborhood is in a peripheral zone and people here want to keep the neighborhood as serene looking as possible.

I will write as often as possible to keep you informed and to let you know I'm okay. Hope you care but I don't want you to worry. I love you very deeply and do wish we could be together now and always. But as things are, we must just keep faith in one another and wait. I must admit that I am impatient. But I would be satisfied to just hold you in my arms and feel the closeness of your beautiful being. I need that very much. I hope you are going to be the cuddly type.

Good-bye for now. Be beautiful and be happy. I cannot imagine you any other way. All my thoughts and love are with you tonight.

Forever,
Duane

19

My Proposal

After a week, I receive a call from Dr. McDaniels saying that it is safe for me to return to campus. I have fallen behind not only in my classes but also in my research for term papers as I've been unable to go to the library. I don't expect to be threatened as a white man on campus but understand that their anger and grief over the assassination of Dr. King is still raw.

After the time off mourning for Dr. King and waiting for things to settle down, I find myself trying to catch up at the library in the evenings after hours. Focused on taking notes, the library janitor interrupts and quietly says, "Mr. Johnson, there are two policemen that want to see you at your car in the parking lot."

I head to the parking lot in somewhat of a panic. There are two policemen standing by my car shining their flashlights probing the inside of the glass. As I approach, the larger cop asks, "Is this your car?"

I respond, "Yes, sir."

The cop says, "What the hell is it doing in the Atlanta U library parking lot?"

I say, "I was inside doing research. I'm a graduate student and haven't had access because of the death and funeral of Dr. King."

"Well, someone doesn't like you! They cut one of your tires. Do you have a driver's license?"

I reach into my pocket, shakily flip through my wallet, and pull out my license.

"What the hell? This is for Montana and your car is licensed in Georgia. What the hell are you doing down in Atlanta, Georgia with Georgia plates on your car and no Georgia driver's license?"

I explain, "I'm a graduate student and I bought the car here and have not had time to get a Georgia driver's license."

They ask me to stand behind my car while they discuss the situation. The big guy tells me, "Go back inside and study while we go and get the tire fixed. We'll be back once the tire is fixed."

The janitor greets me by the desk I was using earlier, "What's all that about, Mr. Johnson?"

"Somebody slashed one of my tires and police are going to see if they can get it fixed."

"They're good cops," the janitor says, "I told them you are a good person. They probably already know all about you."

About two hours later accompanied by another patrol car, a new cop is standing by my car which has been taken off the jack, and announces, "Mr. Johnson, let me give you some advice. Don't ever park your car in or around this neighborhood. And I'd find another library to do your research."

"Yes sir."

"You got a brand-new tire gratis of the city of Atlanta. It won't cost you more than a thank you note to the parish commander letting him know what you told us and what we did for you. Right now, you should go home—goodbye."

On Saturday night, I treat myself to dinner out after being cooped up in my little apartment. It is a great night, listening to a live band while savoring my dinner and drink. The next morning, however, is not that good as I'm in terrible pain after puking all night. I crawl over to Mrs. Bennett's door and lightly rap on it. She answers and after one look at me, she exclaims, "You look horrible. What happened?"

I grab my stomach and double over with pain. "I think I ate some bad food."

Immediately, she says, "Let me call a taxi to rush you to the hospital."

After waiting for one hour to see the emergency room doctor, I try to explain, "I think I'm going to die." They finally decide they need to move quickly and start asking me questions, "Where did you go? What did you eat?"

They check my vitals; find I'm dehydrated and place me on an IV. After running tests, they explain that I have food poisoning and will have to stay in the hospital for two nights.

Although, I feel weak and don't have an appetite, I return to my apartment feeling pressure to study for mid-term exams. My exams start in mid-May and then I'll be busy writing my thesis. I also plan to take three courses in Manpower Development during the summer. I have explained this to Loretta as I won't have the time to write letters. I tell her that I'll try to call regularly. I have to admit that I'm surprised that Loretta is now chasing me. I'm not sure what has changed but it's a pleasant surprise after chasing her in January and her being as cool as a cucumber. Things hadn't worked out for her to come to Atlanta in March as I had messed up on my vacation days. She tells me that her parents are buying her a round-trip ticket to Atlanta in June for a graduation present.

My schedule looks as though I'll be done by August 1st if all goes well. Gordon Hoven, an attorney with the Economic Development Administration in Havre and a friend of Frank Hayes, (my supervisor last summer) has informed me of a position opening in Montana—it offers $11,000 a year. If necessary, I will fly up for an interview. I also have offers to stay in Atlanta and other cities in the South ... I'm still considering them. One is in Tampa Bay but I'd only accept it if Loretta is willing to teach there. She has concerns because their education system has had sanctions in prior years caused by insufficient financing. Loretta has been undecided about our future so it's hard for me to make plans. I think she wants to stay in Montana or Washington State, although there seems to be a good chance that she may be finalizing a contract to teach in Oregon.

Term papers and writing my thesis help the time fly. Loretta graduates from Montana State University on June 7, 1968 and catches a flight out of Bozeman the next day. She's a novice flyer and the ticketing agents in Bozeman misguide her. They said that she'd have enough time in St. Louis to claim her bag (ninety minutes) and recheck it to Atlanta. She is flying on Frontier Airlines through Denver en route to St. Louis. Sadly, between mechanical problems in Denver and thunderstorms on the way to St. Louis, she is left with only five minutes to get off the plane, collect her bag, and get to the next gate. She nearly faints on the tarmac in St. Louis as she tries to run to baggage claim, from the ninety-eight-degree temperature with ninety-five percent humidity.

I had big plans with a party for her at Bruce's house since she was due to arrive at 7:30 p.m. She finally connects with me and says that the earliest connection won't get her to Atlanta until 5:00 a.m. Disappointed, I tell her that I can't pick her up and that she should take a taxi to the Peachtree Hotel. She understands but is unaware that I'm leading her on. Instead, I stand outside her gate and as she gets off the plane she's thrilled and relieved to see me.

We spend a wonderful week together and she experiences big city life in Atlanta. I take her to Atlanta University but she huddles down on the floorboard afraid to look around because she's afraid that people will think she's staring at them.

Taken aback by the ramifications of living in a large city, Loretta is amazed that we need to leave one hour early to beat the traffic rush. She has her first experience at a Chinese restaurant tasting sweet and sour shrimp. She's impressed by our elegant dinner at the Lion's Head. Another first was having Drambuie for an after-dinner drink. We teasingly bet about the cost only to have a liquor store validate the cost. I decide that a bottle of Drambuie isn't in my budget so we settle for a reasonably priced champagne.

This leads to an intimate conversation, and finally I ask, "Loretta, will you marry me?"

She says, "Yes! I only wish that you could come home with me now!"

Wednesday, April 24, 1968

Hi Sugar,

Well, it has been so long since the last time I wrote I think I might have forgotten how. No kidding, I just kept putting it off until now it is an absolute must.

I just got back from meeting with Dr. Williams. We had a long discussion about Tampa Bay, Florida. He finally asked me what I thought about it...and I said 'great!' But...and then I told him about you not wanting to teach down there. He thought that the sanction had been lifted and that Florida was rapidly improving its education system. After a bit longer, he tried to pin me down again, and I told him 'no,' but thanks a lot. Loretta, I just cannot see me living in the South. There are so many things that remind me of bigotry and pre-judgement here in the South. It goes beyond disgust for me. No job, or any amount of money makes it worthwhile. So, now I have to get on the ball and find something in the Northwest. I bet you think I'm nuts...for changing my mind and all but I thought you were a little negative about Florida and if I'm correct I think you want to live in either Washington or Montana.

Hey...I'm high. We had a couple Manhattans and wow, can you tell? Just my typing has gotten a little worse. Loretta, you have to appreciate how I feel right now. I haven't had much to drink for so long that I really am in no shape to handle booze anyway. And on top of that I have been dieting. Eating nothing but eggs, grapefruit and cottage cheese. I did not need to go on a diet but I quit smoking and was afraid that I would gain a lot of weight. So, I put myself on this diet until my metabolism settles down. You would not know me. I weigh 130...and hope to get down to 120. (Give or take 30 lbs.)

Kid, I hope you are not upset by how I pressured you about the future. But it is hard for me to sit and write and tell you a lot of garbage if it isn't going to mean something in the future. Actually, I think it is stupid for us to think that we love each other right now. We don't even know each other...how can we talk about love? But I think that our discussion proved one thing...that at least we are not interested in someone else. I am now hoping that I will have the chance to let you get to know me and that I can learn to know you and that we have not been wrong about each other.

Not much of a letter is it? Well, I'm tired and feel smashed. I have a statistic test next week plus a term paper that is due so *this weekend will be hell. I might call if you're in, but don't plan on writing.*

I think about you very much. 'Till later. X – here's that smooch you wanted. Love ya, Sweet Pea! Wow, I bet I am in trouble now. First from writing a short and senseless letter and then ending it by getting smart. If I didn't know that you are good natured, I would be worried.

Much love,
Duane

May 6, 1968

Dear Loretta,

Just a short note to let you know I can keep a promise. No real news to report, but lots of activity at school which will not interest you. This looks like another big week. I can hardly believe there are only three big ones left. I will really have to get busy if I'm going to pass the comprehensives. I guess a lot of guys have to come back in a year and retake them. In the meantime, they cannot get any action on their thesis.

I wrote Bob Kaste a letter yesterday. I might be able to see him or maybe if he gets a pass he can come to Atlanta. Well, no big deal.

Loretta, I am amazed by your attitude towards me. When I was 'chasing' you and wanting to talk marriage you were as cool as a cucumber; now, I have been gone for almost nine months and you somehow seemed to have changed your mind. Why? Are you forgetting about your 'faith' and your parents? I am not trying to sound negative or doubtful but I would like to have you explain why the change of heart. I am still 'me!'

Oh well, nothing to worry about, I guess. They say women have a greater propensity to change their minds. If you have a reason though, please write them down and send them to me...I'm interested.

See what happens when I try to write a letter when I have nothing to say. But at least you can chalk one more up. I am about to finish a dreadful theory book...I will be up all night. But I don't have any day classes tomorrow so I'll make it.

Must run...play it cool...and 'YOU' smile.

As ever,
Duane

20

The End

I'm beginning to see that the end is possible and busy myself studying for final exams. I have had the blues since Loretta left and lack motivation. Pounding out the last two term papers provides some relief.

I spend $68.00 (a fortune for me) to have the MG tuned up so it's ready for the road trip ahead. My plan is to leave on August 10th and I anticipate a four-day drive home.

Dr. Cothran has been pressuring me to take a position within the department since I'm the only one that has not committed to an agency. The position is as an administrative assistant, which sounds important, until I talk to the person that holds that position now. He is about ready to crack from taking so much guff. I tell Dr. Cothran, "Thanks, but I am planning to commit to a position in Montana." I choose not to tell him that Loretta has signed a contract for a teaching position in Oakridge, Oregon and she is wanting me to find a position in Eugene or Portland, Oregon near her.

I successfully defend my research design for my thesis, (A Study of the Self-Concept on the Long-Term Unemployed) before the full body of sociology students and faculty. Not surprisingly, the questions are mostly from the students and concern how I've articulated the Negro population per the preponderance in the universe of poverty. Some students seem compelled to try and get me to say *Nigra*. One of the faculty, not on my thesis committee, finally interrupts, "Mr. Johnson will make, if needed, any corrections while finishing his thesis."

While I recall anxious anticipation on my arrival in Atlanta, I will never forget the horror of Friday, August 9th, my last day in the city. I wake up early, anxious to conclude a successful day. I find a place to park on the street. Ironically, it is in front of the main entrance to Ware Hall. The sun is just coming up when I arrive at the library. I visualize my lecture notes and the books I've read to prepare for the final test. The test calls for an understanding of existing problems within the war on poverty: How can we help people rise out of poverty and into the mainstream of the American workforce?

As I approach the test site building, the sun coming over the horizon is breaking through the fog. It appears today will be another hot day, and probably very muggy. Smiling to myself, I'm looking forward to writing my final exam on the Atlanta odyssey. I feel confident and prepared for this final test when suddenly I feel a slimy wetness running down the front of my face. I look up angrily and see a young female student taking credit to an audience of about seven males for the act of spitting on me. I continue on to the test site, and try to calmly convince myself, *this will soon be over, do not overreact to an expression of hate, jealousy, or whatever it's supposed to mean.*

My hands are still shaking when I grab five blue books and read through the requirement on the chalkboard: *Please explain the greatest issues in poverty and what you would do to solve them.* As I fiercely write all the things that come to mind, I hope that all the parts are coming together into a meaningful dialogue. I'm not aware of how high the temperature has risen, until I notice sweat dripping from my chin onto my test paper. Two-and-a-half hours later, I finish. In the five blue books, I've written and

225

expanded upon all the knowledge I've stored and learned during the past year about poverty as we know it in the United States. As I leave the test site, I have never felt so insecure, and force myself from returning to make sure that my name and number are on each of the blue books.

I then head for my car and find another vehicle in the space where I left my MG GT! Dazed, I look up and down the row of parked cars when Bruce walks up.

"Duane, we did it … aren't you glad that's over?" he comments.

I reply, "My car is missing!"

"You mean it was stolen?" he questions.

"Yeah," I say.

"You better report it to the police right away. I'll give you a ride to your apartment."

When I get to my apartment, I survey the books and clothes that I need to stuff into my duffle bag and one hard-sided suitcase. I wonder how I'll get the bags and my typewriter to the airport. Deciding that I'll worry about that later, I call the police. I'm despondent when they indicate, "You will probably never see your car again. We have car gangs working the southwest side of Atlanta!"

I mentally try to remember who has a car and automatically dial Ware Hall. The switch board operator connects me with the second floor where Hector picks up. Unfortunately, he can't think of anyone other than Lonnie and he hasn't seen him around the dorm. "Thanks, man. I gotta go."

I then look through my address book and the only home phone number that makes sense is Arthur Askew's, a fellow worker at the Atlanta Employment Evaluation & Service Center. Luckily, he's home and as he answers, I plead, "Arthur, I need some help."

"How so?" he asks.

"When I came out of my test this morning, my car was missing. I called the police but I don't feel very optimistic that I'll ever see it again."

"It will take about forty-five minutes to get to your apartment and I can take you to the airport. Have you got a ticket yet?" he asks in his usual calm voice.

After a while, Arthur pulls up in his station wagon and asks, "Where's all your stuff?"

"This is it—I just have a duffle bag and one suitcase, and my type-writer that I'm going to keep out."

"No sweat, let's get this stuff in the back. What airline, Johnny?"

"I think the best route to Montana is via St. Louis, Billings, and then on to Great Falls on United."

"I'll let everyone at the center know what's happened. We'll be anxious to hear if you make it home okay," Arthur says as we reach United's ticketing area. Arthur waits with me until my one-way ticket has been issued. He then says, "Well, Johnny you're on your way home to Loretta and your beloved Montana. You've been a good friend. Call and let me know once you make it home."

Wednesday, July 3, 1968

Hi Sweetheart,

Hi. Well, I'm still alive but not very. I have been on an excursion to the 'happy hunting grounds' but didn't like what I saw so came back. I was so sick Sunday until this morning. I really did think I was gonna die. My landlady called a taxi and sent me to an emergency doctor Sunday night. At the hospital,

*they found that I had food poisoning. Some vegetable that I had
eaten was bad. That's what you get from eating in restaurants.
But today I think I have shaken it and feel great. But I have
really lost weight. I guess I will have to drink lots of beer so I
won't make you look bad when I see you again.*

*Well, I finally got financial backing to write this letter. I know
it is long overdue but I hope it reaches you and reinforces the
'good-guy' image.*

*We have a little break over this weekend…but then we go back
to a set of mid-term exams. The last time for mid-terms. This
has been the most miserable semester so far. I seem to have
the blues and all I think about is my little sweetie…. Really, I
do miss you; I hope I can make it. I have more than once just
about climbed in the ole MG and headed Big Sandy way. Also,
another factor is that I have all my requirements out of the way
and feel little motivation to hit the books.*

*Herman (the rat) has been giving me a lot of trouble since you
left. I warned him if he didn't change his ways, I wouldn't take
him with me. The little rebel told me he didn't want to come.
He says he has heard some bad tales about Big Sandy. Besides
he is mad because I made him take his rebel flag down. Guess
I'm just hard to get along with.*

*I had the MG tuned up and ready for travel. It cost me 68
dollars for the tune-up. I just about flipped but I guess it pays in
the long run. The little bug had better not give me any trouble
on the road…that's all I can say.*

*I have gotten myself in a jam with the printer's union. I kept
a traveling card out too long and didn't pay my dues on time.*

The darn thing really had just slipped my mind until I thought that I might have to pick up a few shifts until I find a position that is suitable. I guess it will cost me a couple hundred dollars to square it away. It (the case) has to go to international headquarters to be reviewed. I really feel like a deviant. That has been the biggest trouble I've been in for a long time. I don't stay in practice like you do.

The head of the department has been pressuring me about taking a position with the department. I am about the only one that has not committed himself to an agency somewhere. The job is administrative assistant. Sounds important, but is really nothing more than a high-class errand boy. The pay is lousy, and the guy that holds the position now is just about ready to crack up. I guess he gets a lot of guff. I told him, "Thanks, but no thanks."

I called Great Falls to see if they had anything on Oregon. Guess who I talked to...you probably already know...your big sister. She said she would mail the address of the State Employment Office for Oregon. I (now see what you made me do) now have to use another sheet of my stationery. As I was saying, young lady, I hope by now that you realize that I have a very special kind of love and respect for you. It's not the kind that you describe on a typewriter. I do hope you are aware of it when we are close and that the time comes soon when we can be close.

Honey, I get nervous when I start talking that way, especially when you're not by my side to reassure me that I should. Please have faith...I'm on my way. You will probably see me riding across the prairie on my horse and in my favorite cow-hat.

I'm really anxious to go down to the Vets Club and make that announcement. I hope this time you will keep your elbow out of my mouth.

Be seeing you soon good-looking. Until then, I remain

Affectionately yours,
Duane

Saturday, July 6, 1968

Dear Loretta,

Hi Good-looking! I had better use up the last of my exquisite cowboy paper to write and let you know that all is "OK." I hope the shock of receiving two letters so close together won't be too much for you.

I am just about to start writing my second-to-last term paper. I didn't want to chance anything happening to the typewriter, so thought I would write you first. (Brack...at times like this, I can hardly stand myself.)

Last night I took a break and went to a movie. It was a western, starring Dean Martin and James Stewart. It was really great. They talked about going to Missoula, Montana, to get a fresh start. Wow, did I get homesick. The dialogue got a little rough in places, so I wouldn't advise you seeing it. Besides, you got your own cowboy coming home in four weeks.

With just four weeks left in school, the schedule is getting pretty tight. I'm afraid there won't be any time for 'breaks' from here on in. I hope the weather doesn't get too hot so I can get some studying done. And Heaven knows, I have some to get done.

I hope to leave on the tenth of August and hit Great Falls on the 14ᵗʰ. I don't like the idea of starting off on a weekend but I will cool it and push the little bug as gently as I can. Maybe on the 16ᵗʰ, 17ᵗʰ, or 18ᵗʰ we can get together with everyone and have a barbeque or something. I hope Dave and Marj are still there when I arrive. I hope LaVern gets the new album by Johnny Cash at Folsom Prison. I am anxious to hear it...and I'm so poor now that I won't be able to buy it until it's out of date.

Sweetheart, I hope everything is all right with you. I hope you don't get too excited about this job in Oregon and start having accidents. Just play it cool...no, don't do that either. The last time you tried to be cool (with your little dance) you landed on your head. Try not to do too much of anything until I'm there to watch over you.

I'm nasty, and I know it. Loretta, I'm afraid I don't have a lot of news to report. It's the same old drag. Beer, girls and parties... you know how it is for us grad students. I will be so glad to settle down to work and all.

Well kid, time is flying. I hope to be home soon. Take care. That's the last of my stationery. Guess I will not need any more stamps. Loretta – be good et be mine.

Love,
Me

July 6, 1968

Dear Folks,

Just a note to let you know that I'm still alive…and that's about all. With less than four weeks left of school the schedule is getting pretty tight. I have two term papers left to do and lots of studying for the finals. But the tighter the schedule, the faster time flies.

I took a break last night and went to a movie. It was a western, with Dean Martin and James Stewart and called Bandolero! They talked about going to Missoula, Montana, to get a fresh start, and brother, did I get homesick. The longer I stay down here, the more intense is my dislike for the whole place.

Loretta called and informed me that she has signed a contract to teach in Oakridge, Oregon. She would like for me to find a position near there. I like the area, so will give it a stab. It is only 35 miles from Eugene and about 100 miles from Portland. It is above the 'fog banks' and below the snow level. Sounds great…and yeah, it's 80 miles from the coast. Well, I'll give it a look.

I took an honorable withdrawal from the Typographical Union last week. I just couldn't hack these thirty-dollar monthly union dues, especially when I'm not working. I can go back to work by just depositing the withdrawal card and ten dollars. If I had known that I would have done that last fall and saved myself a couple of hundred dollars. Like Pa says, "You either gotta keep your eyes open, or your pocketbook open." I got caught with my eyes closed.

I have fallen behind the self-imposed schedule I wanted to follow for the writing of my thesis. My advisor is a little disappointed in me too. He thought I was going to break all records and get my degree from this lousy place in nine months. I hope to at least finish it by Christmas, which is still pretty good time. I ran into complications testing a control group and then when Loretta came down, I lost a couple of weeks. But the real truth is that I just ran out of steam.

The weather has been great the last couple of days—about low 80 degrees. Yesterday, it felt so good to be in bed with covers on that I actually stayed there until 2:30 in the afternoon. But it's warming up again!

I can't think of a heck of a lot of news. I am getting a little anxious to get out of here. I never paid so much attention to the passing days since I was in the Army. When August ninth comes around, I will be one hell-of-a relieved guy. I plan to leave about the tenth and it will probably take me four days to make Great Falls so keep an eye open. That's it for now.

I hope all are in good health! Hope the weather is nice enough to have a barbecue when I get home—so I can have an excuse to drink lots of beer. Maybe, I'll get to see that 'lost' sister of mine. Take care.

Love and Respect,
Duane

P.S. I got my grades for last semester—4 A's. Yeah, you can be no more surprised than I was. I wonder what my old 'friend and counselor' would say to that.

Epilogue

Arriving in Montana, I purchase our longed-for diamond ring formally proposing to Loretta on August 11, 1968. Later in the week, I return from shopping and Dad says, "Duane, the Atlanta Police Department called and they want to hear from you as soon as possible. They have located your MG GT and it is in Police Impoundment tallying a charge of $50 a day." I am shocked!

I place a call to the Police Department and listen to their request. "Y'all better get down here and get your car 'fore you can't afford to pay. We won't give you your car 'til these fees are paid up. You have 'til August 15th to clear up your debt and keep it from going on the public auction block no later than September 1st."

I explain, "My father, Robert Johnson, will pay my fees and I give permission to release the car to him." I indicate to a patient and understanding police officer, "I promised to move my fiancée and her clothes to her teaching position in Oregon".

My Dad is coaching me on the side, while I negotiate with the police officer, "I will volunteer to get your car as I always wanted to drive across the U.S. I will fly out of Great Falls on the earliest flight. Just get the address and I will take care of your business."

Meanwhile, my Dad graciously loans me his car to transport Loretta and her clothing to Oakridge, Oregon, helping her move into an acceptable apartment. Little did we know that the car only left the garage for weddings or funerals, never for a highway trip. As we approach Coeur d' Alene, Idaho – a city known for weddings with no waiting period, Loretta asks, "What does the red light on the dashboard mean?"

"Oh, damn it!" I utter. We limp into the first exit and see a Union 76 gas station. We soon learn the car is going to have to spend the night and wait to have a new alternator installed. The owner lends us extra noisy 1939 Chevrolet pickup, Loretta requires a step-stool for access.

The following day, August 20, 1968 finds us in line purchasing our marriage license. The $25 wedding package offers everything we need, a justice of the peace, a slightly over-weight woman running back and forth being our bridesmaid/witness, in between playing the organ and throwing the rice. The justice of the peace, amazed that we have a beautiful diamond and wedding bands, cracks a smile when I nervously respond, "With this wing, I thee red."

Loretta cracks up laughing and struggles to contain herself. Our package includes a wedding cake, Loretta eager to get our money's worth, puts in her order which I proceed to squelch as soon as we notice a teenage couple receiving a cupcake with a lit sparkler.

Later our marriage with our three-year-old daughter in attendance, is blessed in the Big Sandy Catholic Church to the happiness of Loretta's Mom and Dad.

Securing a position with the Economic Development Administration for Hill County, Rocky Boy and Fort Belknap Indian Reservations fulfills my nine-month obligation working with a poverty agency. With research data gained from 50 individuals at the Atlanta Employment Evaluation & Service Center, I complete my thesis *A Study of the Self-Concept on the Long-Term Unemployed.* Unable to attend my graduation ceremony, graduation with a Masters of Arts in Sociology and an emphasis in Research Methods brings closure to the Atlanta Odyssey. Most of the faculty during my tenure are gone. Some have retired or gained positions with other institutions of higher education. To each and every one of them, I extend my respect and gratitude. Along the way I lose touch with fellow students. The few that stand out in my memory are Robbie Burns, Lonnie Burton, Cy Smith, Hector the Greek, Troy King and Arthur Askew all of from my estimation are contributing in many different ways in solving racism and poverty in the US. My degree, brings a position with OEO in Governor Anderson's Office in Montana and as Associate Professor teaching at my Great Falls alma mater. Obtaining a Master of Science in Industrial Relations in 1974 at the University of Oregon provides for a career of nearly 35 years of contract negotiations representing just and equitable treatment of union members by their owners.

Calls for *Black Lives Matter* and continued concerns about racism are still being felt in 2020. My wife's 50 year-old-love letters have provided me with insight into my thoughts and emotions during my year at Atlanta University. I take a look at the school, the faculty, the neighborhood, Atlanta, and myself. Diversity and how people of different races relate, remain topics of interest not just for governmental agencies, academicians and educational administrators, but also for everyone from CEOs to the first-line supervisors.

I look to a day when people will not be judged by the color
of their skin, but by the content of their character.

Martin Luther King, Jr.

About The Authors

Duane and Loretta celebrated their 50th wedding anniversary on August 20, 2018, with the old adage *It Was Meant to Be!* They have two married daughters and three grandchildren. After extensive travel and numerous moves throughout the Pacific Northwest and Montana, they are currently retired and reside in a suburb of Seattle.

Loretta's debut book, *FARM STORIES – A Fading Dream* was published in 2017 as a memoir.